THERE'S NO BUSINESS LIKE SHOW BUSINESS . . . WAS

BY ALAN YOUNG

THERE'S NO BUSINESS LIKE SHOW BUSINESS . . . WAS
© 2006 Alan Young

PUBLISHED IN THE USA BY:

**BearManor Media
PO Box 71426
Albany, GA 31708
www.BearManorMedia.com**

LIBRARY OF CONGRESS CATALOGING-IN-PUBLICATION DATA:

Young, Alan, 1919-
   There's no business like show business . . . was / by Alan Young.
     p. cm.
  ISBN 1-59393-053-4
  1. Young, Alan, 1919- 2. Actors--United States--Biography. I. Title.

PN2287.Y57A3 2006
791.4502'8092--dc22
                             2006013209

Printed in the United States.

Design and Layout by Valerie Thompson.

TABLE OF CONTENTS

Dedicated to Carol Summers,
whose expertise and management made this book possible.

⧉ INTRODUCTION ⧉
THERE'S NO BUSINESS LIKE
SHOW BUSINESS . . . WAS

The title of this book came to me when I was halfway through writing it. At first it sounded a little condescending so I decided to check it out with a group of people of diverse ages. Amazingly, their reaction was quite positive, in fact one individual responded with an enthusiastic, "Yeah, tell it like it was!"

The continual replaying of old shows, movies and their remakes is now a common phenomenon. Investigating this infatuation with former days, the responses I received indicated that people are not trying to turn to the past, but, rather, they want to have a part of the past come to them, a little like "returning to the future."

In reviewing television today, for example, an amazingly subtle transition is evident; everybody wants to get into the act. In the fifties, a newsman or woman sat in front of a camera and read the news. Today, the events are just about the same, I mean news doesn't alter, it just happens, but our reporting of it is completely different. It now takes two or three people to tell us what's happening, along with several others to write comments, jokes and introductions.

Presidents and senators have gag writers and camera experts to advise them. Politics has become show business, and, in some instances, vice versa. It is communication gone berserk. And, of course, nothing is sacred or subtle. "If it happens, it's our responsibility to show it" seems to be the dictum. The First Amendment is quoted as an excuse for depicting rape, murder, and sexual deviancy as a form of dramatic art. It's not a responsibility they are living up to; it's a lack of writing talent. I guess they just can't think of any other ideas.

In an interview a number of years ago, as I remember, Gregory Peck said, "If I can't communicate to the audience that I love a girl without shoving my tongue down her throat, I don't deserve to be in pictures."

Admittedly, up until the mid-1960s, some of the restrictions in movies and television were unbelievably naive. When a movie showed a U.S. Marine shaking his fist at a strafing Japanese plane and yelling, "Darn you!," it did seem a little unrealistic. In *Gone With the Wind*, Clark Gable's line, "Frankly, my dear, I don't give a damn" was considered by some the height of degradation. In television, twin beds were an absolute must, even if the couple had been married for twenty years and had five children. And you never showed a pregnant woman! It was as if David and Ricky Nelson had been adopted. On *Mister Ed*, my wife and I always slept in twin beds, four feet apart. One day as a gag, the property master and I faked a well-worn path on the carpet between the beds to see what would happen. I don't know if it was never photographed or the censors had a sense of the ridiculous, but there were no repercussions.

In 1962, after seeing a full body shot of my horse, a movement was started by some religious zealot to clothe all the animals on TV, Ed being the prime target! These extremes are ridiculous, of course, but it does seem as if the pendulum has swung so far the other way that it's knocked a hole in our morals.

Is it any wonder that a person like me, and there are many I am sure, begins to recall those days ("olden" children call them) with a certain sigh? Not a sigh of nostalgia, because that in itself is a mournful reaction.

No, mankind's progression and improvement are inevitable and welcome. The rosy future is implicated in the bright present. But somehow along the line, while we were donning the fresh, glorious garments of advancement, we dropped our pants.

This is Ed and me responding to one fan who requested all TV animals be clothed. Do you agree?

The following stories about show business are not an attempt to return to the "glorious" Hollywood past. I'm sure my black brothers would have something to say about that. There was nothing glamorous for them being on the outside and sometimes not being able to even look in, unless it was to don a maid's apron or a chauffeur's cap.

I am attempting to remind myself and others of the heritage we have in this great occupation. We have a precious legacy of partnership, enthusiasm and love of the craft which, in many cases, seems to have been dropped along the way. It is my hope that these remembrances may awaken in each of us the fact that this vocation that has chosen us is a precious one, involving obligations on our part if it is to continue.

None of the following accounts is apocryphal. I witnessed most of them first-hand. The stories may be unbelievable, but in those days — so was show business!

⤞ CHAPTER ONE ⤝
RADIO — THE SIMPLE LIFE!

In 1945 ABC broadcast a series called *The Philco Hall of Fame* with the famous bandleader Paul Whiteman as host. Each week they invited stars who were performing on stage, or had a new motion picture to promote. I was appearing in my comedy show in Toronto, Canada and was amazed to receive a call asking if I would care to be on the program. It was a big-time broadcast and I quickly accepted. When I arrived at the theater where the show broadcast and found it was one of Broadway's oldest and

My first radio show in America — Vocalist Bea Wain — 1948.

This photo was taken right after we said to each other "You haven't changed a bit!" 2006.

most famous houses, I was panicky. Then when I saw the script I was puzzled, panicky and petrified. I could hardly understand a word of it. The New York names such as Pitkin Avenue, and colloquialisms such as "yer fadder's moustache," totally escaped me.

The others on the show included Tallulah Bankhead, who was to do a scene from her latest picture *Lifeboat*. Zero Mostel was there because he was the latest rage in the nightclub circuit. I think I was there because I was the only Canadian comedian they'd ever heard of.

I rehearsed my material and the combination of jokes I barely understood; together with my Canadian-Scottish accent, I sounded like I was speaking Esperanto. I finished my bit and sat down to a wild wave of total disinterest. Next, Tallulah began rehearsing her scene from *Lifeboat*, and suddenly there was a little disturbance coming from the empty theater. Zero was sitting in the third row with some friends, and when he thought of a funny bit and had an

Always alert and ready.

audience, he couldn't resist doing a routine. This time he should have resisted the temptation.

Tallulah stopped her dialogue, walked to the stage apron and speared Zero with an accusatory finger. Then she spewed out a vitriolic diatribe in language I had only heard from a Canadian lumberjack. Now I really wanted to go home. She finished her scene, then sat down beside me and smiled pleasantly. "Enjoying New York?" she asked.

"It's a lovely city," I said.

She patted me on the hand. "Don't feel too badly. You'll be back in Canada very soon."

That's not exactly what I wanted to hear, but I could tell she spoke the truth.

Explaining my jokes to the sergeant in 1946.

"My sketch is a disaster, isn't it?" I asked.

"I wouldn't say it was that good," she replied. "But don't worry. You're very young, you come across charmingly and you'll get a lot of sympathy."

Then she began to tell me of her visit to Victoria and how much she delighted in the gentleness of the people and enjoyed having tea and biscuits served on fine china. All this from a woman who only minutes before had been verbally flaying Zero like a drill sergeant. My part in the program was dreadful, and I left New York a sadder but not much wiser young man. However, I had met and worked with my first American star and learned a lot from her honesty and kindness — and I also learned a lot of new words!

Between Jane Wyman and Olga San Juan, I could have stayed there forever.

In 1948, Alan Young and Bill Thompson (the first Scrooge McDuck), taught a then unknown Marilyn Monroe, how to play the pipes.

In the days of radio, a sponsor would commission his advertising agency to purchase 52 weeks of network time and create a program. In the case of radio comedians, it was difficult for the performer to fill all 52 weeks, so his or her contract was for 39 programs and the other 13 weeks were considered as "summer replacement." In spite of my unfortunate debut in American radio,

I was hired six months later as Eddie Cantor's summer fill-in. I arrived in New York again wide-eyed and scared stiff. I had listened to Eddie Cantor's radio program through my childhood years, as he was one of NBC's top stars, and here I was substituting for him.

After my first show I was in the lobby, meeting the crowd and doing the required handshakes. A very pretty young lady came up to me and shook my hand saying, "I loved your program. I'm an actress, and I would give anything, I mean anything to be on your show."

I suddenly felt her left hand run down my fly. "My God," I thought. "My fly still has buttons. The Americans have zippers! She's going to have a problem getting whatever she wants a hold of."

I gasped, "I don't run the show. My manager is right over there. He hires everybody."

Without hesitation, she left me quicker than it took for her intentions to reach my mind, though not soon enough for it to reach other, more responsive members of my anatomy. (They were always faster than my mind.) I saw her walk up to my manager and perform the same verbal and physical approach. His wife was nearby and he simply smiled, gave her his card and looked away. She turned, smiled at me and left. I never saw her on my show so I figured that her hand, or her follow–up, belied her acting ability.

There was no such thing as videotaping at that time, so we did a show at eight o'clock for the Eastern and mid-American audiences, and then did a repeat show for the West Coast at 11 P.M. The eight o'clock show was fairly well attended but getting an audience in New York at eleven at night, particularly if it was raining, was quite a chore. I remember a few times, we performed in front of two rows of my agent's family members who had been drafted to help out and laugh at anything. And that's the way it sounded.

I had never met Eddie Cantor, so it was a great thrill when he came to New York and agreed to guest on my show. The first

My New York fan club in 1948.

broadcast went well because, even though it was raining, we had a full house. The evening show was another story. When I went out to do the "warm-up" my heart hit my loafers when I saw only two sparsely filled rows. They weren't even family and they looked wet and miserable. Even my warm-up, filled with tried-and-true material, was not only flopping, but was meeting with a mild wave of resentment.

Suddenly the side door opened and in walked a jubilant Eddie Cantor. "Got an audience for you, Alan!" he called, and behind him flocked about two hundred happy people.

During the vocal number in the middle of my show, I discovered how he did it. I was standing backstage with Eddie when an NBC page came in with a bouquet of flowers and a note for Mr. Cantor. "Thanks for making my opening show a memorable one, Mr. Cantor," it said, and it was signed "Jo Stafford."

Jo's program, *The Chesterfield Supper Club*, was broadcast in the studio across the hall. It was only a fifteen-minute radio show, but one of the highlights was the presentation Jo was going to give for the audience and sponsors when they went off the air. It seems that Eddie had stood in the wings until her broadcast was over, then walked on stage, much to the delight of the audience, and the surprise of Jo Stafford.

"Did you enjoy this show?" Eddie asked, and the audience responded with a loud "Yes!"

"Would you like to see another one?" he asked.

"Yes!" they responded, even more enthusiastically.

"Then follow me!" Eddie called, and headed for the audience door. Two hundred people got up and took off, leaving a forlorn and helpless Jo Stafford alone on the stage trying to explain this to her new sponsors. Eddie told me later that when he didn't have an audience in Hollywood for his 5:00 show he would walk up to the Broadway department store on the corner of Hollywood and Vine, climb up on the nearest counter, do a little routine until he attracted a crowd, then lead them two blocks into the studio. He called it the "Pied Piper bit"!

I learned a lot from those old performers. Some good, some I wouldn't care to try.

CHAPTER TWO

HOLLYWOOD: THE BREEDING GROUND
OF CHARACTER — AND CHARACTERS

Sol Brewer (I've changed his name because he's still around) had established himself as one of the ten top successful Hollywood film producers. He had started in show business just after World War II, purchasing inexpensive foreign-made films, adding subtitles and "four walling." This simply meant that he rented a theater or hall for the night and showed his product. As there was no distributor or studio to pay, the profits were all his. Of course, this could be a disaster if improperly handled, but Sol was a genius at production and promotion.

In no time at all ol' Brewer's name was spoken on a par with Goldwyn, Mayer and the other film giants, with as much respect and perhaps more affection. His life was full and complete until he joined Hillcrest Country Club. There he would meet and compare notes with his peers in the business. He could always hold his own and more when the discussion was on business problems and successes, but when the conversation became more social, he was uncomfortable.

Oh sure, he learned to light a cigar and, though he didn't smoke, he could gesture with it and blow smoke with the best of them. He didn't drink either, but he learned to nurse a brandy like a toper. It was when the conversation drifted into the subtle business of extramarital pastimes that Sol was in isolation. One by one they would bemoan, albeit proudly, the problems of keeping a mistress. As they went on and on Sol would smile knowingly, puff his cigar, swill his snifter, but add nothing to the conversation. Finally, he could stand it no longer. He called in his assistant, a knowledgeable, trustworthy and street-smart Hollywood High graduate.

"How do you start an affair?" he asked bluntly.

"Oh it's simple," his assistant said. "You open with the National Anthem, then Hatikva, and then . . ."

"I don't mean that kind of affair," Sol interrupted impatiently. "I want to keep a woman."

The assistant was speechless. Trustworthy, faithful Sol, who had turned down more actresses' advances than Tommy Tune, now wants a mistress? He was soon assured that Sol had no adulterous intentions. He didn't even want to meet the girl, he simply wanted to take on the responsibility so he would know what he was talking about at the Club.

An appreciative young actress was approached and jumped at the opportunity. The apartment was bought and the young lady ensconced. To this day, and we're talking over two years ago, Sol has seen neither the girl nor her apartment, but he is no longer left out of the extracurricular conversation. He can now join his peers in complaining about the extra costs of a Brentwood apartment, diamond watches and lingerie, still pronouncing it "ling-ar-ee." The provocative thought is that somewhere in a Brentwood apartment a young actress sits waiting and wondering.

<hr/>

In 1948 Cy " . . . . . ." was one of Hollywood's hottest new writers. He had two screenplays to his credit and had created a hit radio show. Success meant little to Cy as creature comforts and material possessions were low on his agenda. However, when he visited his friends their newfound wealth was immediately expressed in lavish homes, dress, and of all things Cy was unfamiliar with — art! Not art that Cy recognized, like the Mona Lisa, or Toulouse Lautrec (he'd seen the movie three times), and all the really "good" stuff. But his friends went into rapture leading him from room to room pointing out all their Neo and Nuovo acquisitions.

And it wasn't just one of his friends, it was *all* of them! Some had statuary that resembled his uncle's junkyard back in Queens. His boyhood friend Artie, whose only artistic possession until last year was a collection of New York Rangers hockey cards, was now in exaltation over a six-foot-square white-on-white oil titled "Snowstorm in Minsk."

"And they gave it away for only ten thou," he smirked knowingly. "Obviously they didn't know what they had. But I did!"

"It's terrific, Artie," said Charlie, now writing for Fox.

Mort, recently made an associate producer at Paramount, stepped back a few feet to study the white-on-white a little more in depth. "It has a tremendously . . . primitive feel," he said. "A little reminiscent of the Herschell Bagliani I bought last week. It's a study in brown — the Hanging Gardens of Babylon from underneath. I stole it for fifteen thousand."

And so it went, "ooing and aahing" over cubism, dadaism, pre-ismism. Cy neither appreciated nor understood their collections but he recognized the status message, and he decided if you can't join 'em, lick 'em.

A month later, Cy's friends received an invitation for cocktails to view his latest acquisition. His apartment walls were bare except for a small frame lit by two baby-spots. His friends crowded around the hanging object and were transfixed.

Behind the non-glare glass was a triangular stamp with one of the corners slightly damaged. But all eyes were devouring a newspaper clipping which was fixed below the stamp. It read:

"DATELINE RHODESIA — A ONE KRONER STAMP WAS RECENTLY SOLD BY TRANSVAAL ANTIQUITIES FOR TEN THOUSAND POUNDS. THIS IN ITSELF IS NO GREAT WONDER AS THE STAMP IS 1850 AND EXTREMELY RARE.

"THE UNBELIEVABLE FACT IS THAT THE STAMP IS SLOWLY BEING EATEN UP BY THE METISQUI MIDGE, A MICROSCOPIC ARTHROPOD, INVISIBLE TO THE NAKED EYE. IT IS FELT THAT THE VERMIN WAS ATTRACTED BY THE STAMP'S GLUE, BUT A CLOSE EXAMINATION SHOWS THAT THE ENTIRE STAMP IS BEING DEVOURED.

"INASMUCH AS AUTHORITIES BELIEVE THAT WITHIN FIVE YEARS THIS RARE STAMP WILL BE ALMOST COMPLETELY DESTROYED, CURATORS AT THE ANTIQUITIES WERE AMAZED WHEN A HOLLYWOOD WRITER, WHO DECLINED TO SPEAK TO US, RECENTLY PURCHASED THE STAMP FOR ONE HUNDRED THOUSAND AMERICAN DOLLARS."

Cy was in. He had topped them all. The Hollywood nouveau riche and social elite clamored for invitations to view this wonder of wonders. "Someday I'll tell them," thought Cy. "But not yet."

He would tell them that he bought the stamp for fifty cents, chewed a corner off, then wrote the newspaper clipping, had it printed, aged, then framed. Of course, he never did tell anyone because the object d'art became so famous.

I'm told that people still go to view it although the stamp is long gone. All that is left is the clipping and a small pile of chewed paper at the bottom of the frame.

<hr>

In the following story only the man's name has been changed, because I can't remember it. Even if I could, I wouldn't use it as he may have family still around Los Angeles, and while the story is in no way derogatory, it may cause embarrassment to his kin. So we'll just call him Mel.

Mel was a successful and respected musical conductor in Hollywood in the thirties and forties, specializing in motion picture studio work. His name graced many top motion pictures and he became regarded as one of the Hollywood insiders.

He was not a particularly handsome man, slightly balding and he had one eye, but his fame, ability and sense of humor made him a welcome guest at anyone's party. At that time, the film work week was six days, so Saturday night was party night for the toiling studio people. Then, as the film folk were much more of a family group, after work, and a relaxing party, they headed for Palm Springs to rest and continue partying on Sunday.

Mel worked soberly and hard all week, composing, arranging, and laying down musical tracks, so on Saturday nights he was ready for a relaxing belt or two. He was a fastidious dresser and proud of his appearance and it always bothered him that when he was tired and had a few drinks his real eye became bloodshot while the glass one stayed pristine and shiny white.

This discrepancy troubled his esthetic soul. He finally convinced his optometrist to create two or three glass eyes with a gradation of red-veins to duplicate the alcoholic progress of his good eye. He also ordered a fourth replacement, but instead of having an iris and pupil, he had a tiny American flag inserted in their place.

This was not done for laughs alone, but it had a more utilitarian function. Knowing he had a long drive after the Saturday parties, when Mel felt that his liquor consumption had reached the limit, he would remove his glass eye and insert the Stars and Stripes. This told his host and friends, "I've had enough, don't offer any more." It worked perfectly and Mel had no more trouble with overgenerous bartenders.

"No more for Mel," they would announce. "He's flying the flag!"

On one unforgettable Saturday night, Mel partied as usual, then inserted the warning flag to temper his imbibing. He left the party quite sober, but understandably tired, as the hour was late. Halfway to Palm Springs, he found himself dozing off at the wheel and decided that a few minutes sleep was better than running into a tree. At that time of night and forty years ago, Highway 60 was a deserted thoroughfare, so he felt he would not be disturbed.

He swung off the road, drove down a slope and parked in a grove of trees. Then he leaned back and within moments was fast asleep.

The rest of the story came from the Highway Patrol. A young officer, fresh from training, was on one of his first tours of duty — namely, traveling the lonely Highway 60.

In the darkness, he spotted taillights reflecting off the highway. Getting nearer, he saw tire tracks going down the grassy slope, then he spotted Mel's car apparently crashed into a tree. The young rookie parked his motorcycle and cautiously approached the car.

His flashlight picked up the prone figure of a man in the driver's seat. The driver's window was open and the officer shined his light on the motionless face. The man's eyes were shut and the young man reached in and gently opened the eyelids.

One eye stared up at him while the other was proudly flying the Stars and Stripes!

<hr/>

The following story has been repeated many times and in many different ways. Only two days ago I heard it told and the facts were wrong, but the man's enthusiasm was so great I just couldn't correct him. However, this is how it happened, according to Jim Backus, who told it to me when he returned to the studio.

We were making the RKO picture *Androcles and the Lion*, the great Bernard Shaw classic set in Rome at the time when Christians were thrown into the arena to be eaten by lions. Victor Mature played the lead gladiator and Jim was his second-in-command. They carried off this teamwork beautifully as they had both attended the same school, had grown up together, and been friends all along.

We broke for lunch and, as it was a hot day and they were encased in Praetorian Guard uniforms, breastplate, arm guards, leg metals, laced sandals, steel helmet and leather tunics, they decided that, rather than get changed, then change back, they would simply leave their costumes on.

Most of us just ate in the commissary. The food wasn't great but it sufficed. However, not for Jim and Vic. Their eastern-cultured palates demanded a much more diverse menu so off they drove to a restaurant more fitting their educated taste.

Androcles and the Lion, with Jean Simmons, Robert Newton and Jim Backus.

It was a well-respected establishment, catering to business executives, and the sight of two Roman gladiators clanging through the door must have stopped many a fork in midair. It certainly froze the maitre'd momentarily, who quickly regained his composure.

"I'm sorry gentlemen," he sniffed. "You are not . . . er . . . dressed up to our restaurant standard."

Victor Mature did not suffer fools gladly. "What," he asked loudly, "you mean you don't serve men in uniform?"

As it was just after the Korean War and patriotic feelings were running high, our two gladiators ate grandly.

Another quick Mature story. Victor came from a very fine family and had enjoyed a first-class education and upbringing. Now he was finally enjoying the fruits of well-earned Hollywood

Elsa Lanchester objected to having pets in the house.

Victor Mature

success and decided he wanted to had become accustomed. He decided to join the prestigious Los Angeles Athletic Club and made application.

"I'm sorry," he was told by the committee. "The Los Angeles Athletic Club does not accept actors."

Victor's reply was quick and to the point. "I'm not an actor," he said. "And I've got three pictures to prove it!"

Androcles still can't play "Yankee Doodle"!

CHAPTER THREE
HOLLYWOOD PARTIES

I've lived and worked in Hollywood for fifty years. How long? Well, I was just a kid. Uh-huh. Anyway, having worked at a level where I became familiar with popular Hollywood names, who have remained in my memory either as idols or as tremendous achievers, it is now disappointing, if not downright frightening, to find that I seem to be alone in the memories.

Recently, I met with a few friends. They were younger than I, of course, but, then, as I look around, that seems to be the general situation. They were all people who could be classed as above average, at least in the "general knowledge" category. I mean, they could easily make it to the second or third round of *Jeopardy*, I'm sure.

I said to them, "Who was Atwater Kent?" Their answers ranged from "Superman's father" to "Who?"

Whether he invented a type of radio, improved it or just mass-manufactured it, I don't know, but in the forties his name was right up there with Philco and RCA. In any case, after WWII, he ended up with so much money he didn't fill income tax forms anymore. He just asked the Government, "How much do you need?"

With all this fame and affluence, his life was unpretentious. However, he must have been a little unwillingly cloistered as, after his wife passed on, Atwater not only turned over a new leaf, he removed the whole tree, roots and all. He decided to make up for all the parties and fun he had missed. He was now a little too old and conservative to partake of the Hollywood hoopla, but he could sure as hell watch it! In 1945 he hired one of the town's top publicists, Maggie Ettinger, sister of the famous columnist Louella Parsons, and asked her to throw a party to end all parties.

While Maggie was planning a gigantic soiree, Atwater purchased one of the most impressive mansions in the exclusive Bel Air hilltop estate areas. He then began to prepare it for parties.

By the time it was finished, Maggie was ready and the resultant gala was headlines in every paper from the *New York Times* to the *Baghdad Bugle*. Guests were met at the entrance gates, removed from their cars, placed in carriages, rickshaws, sedan-chairs and transported up through the magnificent gardens to the mansion doors, where Nubians and maidens led them to their tables.

The then-popular *Look* magazine sported a full-color cover, quite revolutionary in early postwar journalism. But, then, it had to be in color because it featured the beautiful Lana Turner, clad in a white-rhinestone dress, seated in a howdah, being carried through the garden on a huge elephant, also draped with elegant trappings and with tusks dripping pearl chains.

Maggie was now famous, Hollywood was ecstatic, the press wild, and Atwater Kent was happy. The party became a yearly wingding and invitations were the scarcest and hottest in Hollywood. Those stars who were not invited saved face by leaving town pleading "on vacation."

In 1947, shortly after my arrival in Hollywood, I received an invitation to "the" party. I couldn't believe it. My first picture *Margie* had not turned me into a hot property and my radio show was still struggling for recognition. Then I realized what must have happened.

I had recently hired a young press-agent named Norman Greer. I liked him because he was about my age and had just left the veteran's hospital after recovering from war wounds. He had rented an office in Maggie Ettinger's suites above the Brown Derby on Vine Street. Evidently Maggie liked him for the same reasons I did and I guess she decided to let a ticket slip by. At least that was my reasoning and I didn't bother delving any deeper.

However, the day before the party, tragedy struck. One of my new Hollywood friends was a young student at UCLA who had also just returned from the military and was paying his tuition by taking extra work at the studios.

He had been hired as a "dress-extra," which meant a higher pay, but, unfortunately, Jim didn't have a tuxedo. "Take mine," I said. "My party isn't until Saturday night and this is only Tuesday."

Jim thanked me profusely, took the tux and left for work. His scene was shot in the dance hall of Beverly Hills High; the same hall where *It's a Wonderful Life* was filmed. In the scene, Jimmy Stewart is dancing with his sweetheart when the floor suddenly begins to open up and the dancers fall into the swimming pool below. This was to be the same scenario. Before my friend Jim could think about anything but the extra five dollars he was making, he and my tux went for a bath.

Saturday morning, a chagrined Jim showed up at my door with a dry-cleaning bag in his hand. He had spent the major part of the week taking my suit to cleaners, tailors, and dressmakers in a vain attempt to get it back to its original shape. I unwrapped the package expecting the worst, and got it. My tux hadn't been the most up-to-date style to begin with but now it fit neither date, time nor description. The pool chlorine had turned the original "midnight blue" into a seven o'clock slime. The material had obviously shrunk and the lapels drooped down like dog ears. I tried to put the pants on and the zipper came off in my hands. "I can't go to the party," I decided.

"You *what*?!" screamed my agent when I told him decision. His name was Bert Prager, a delightfully pleasant man who was, at the moment, neither one. He rushed over to my house and threw a tuxedo at me. "You can borrow mine," he said. "No way am I going to see you miss this party. It'll be important for you."

Bert was about five-foot-nine and a hundred and eighty pounds. I was five-eleven and one forty-five. The pants ended up a couple of inches above my shoes and the only way we could get the waist to fit was to wrap it around and pin it at the side. This gave my rear end a decided twist and the large pleat in front hid my fly entirely.

The jacket was another matter. It was a double-breasted model, which made me look like I was wearing a black barrel. However, we found that if I held my hands behind my back and pulled in the slack, then leaned backward, the effect wasn't so bad. The tie fit perfectly, Bert kindly pointed out.

I got to the Kent Estate early so I could enter and get seated before the guests arrived. Clutching the back of my jacket and leaning back made it a little awkward walking, especially up the long steps to the front door, but the staff, evidently surmising I was handicapped, kindly rushed to guide me to my table. There I could sit and relax while my jacket unwound.

Even though I was the first to arrive and was quite early, Atwater Kent was the perfect host. He came in from the greenhouse, where he'd been potting or something, introduced himself and welcomed me.

He was a very humble and friendly man and, though I could tell he didn't know me, he was enamored of everything to do with show business. Finally, he excused himself so he could go upstairs and get dressed. It was then I realized how early I really was.

Anyway, it gave me time to look around this gorgeous room. There must have been thirty or forty tables, each with differing décor, and they were obviously not from furniture rentals. The chairs and tables were permanent fixtures, custom-made for the occasion. The luxurious tables sported monogrammed silver service and each table had a distinctive and gorgeous floral arrangement, surrounded by bottles of wine. Beyond the tables was a commodious dance floor, flanked by a bandstand. I had beaten the band by ten minutes but now they were set up and beginning to play as the guests arrived.

From my vantage point I could see the stars making their entrance and it was thrilling as I recognized the familiar faces;

Jack Benny with Mary Livingstone, George Burns, Edgar Bergen, Rita Hayworth with Orson Welles, famous actresses and actors galore, and all dressed to the nines.

Mercifully, my table was at the back of the room slightly behind a post so I could conceal my sartorial hodgepodge. I know the dinner was served because I ate, but my eyes never left the tables of the stars. To watch them, eating just like normal people, was unbelievable! One of them, a notorious drinker, was already drunk. And I was there!

I had wondered why there was such preponderance of comedians and performers among the stars of the cinema, and after the dinner I discovered why.

Margie, 1946. What do you mean I can't skate?

The lights were dimmed, there was a fanfare and Jack Benny rose and walked to the stage to the accompaniment of enthusiastic applause. He did a terrific monologue, appropriate to the occasion, gave a short violin routine, then introduced George Burns. Naturally, George roasted Jack Benny to the roar of delight from the crowd and the hysteria of Benny. George then introduced Edgar Bergen, who brought Charlie McCarthy up and he, or they, did a sensational five minutes or so.

By now, I had laughed so much I'd sprung the safety pin holding my waistband together, but who cared? I was witnessing show business history, and I'd only been here a few months. Red Skelton was on stage now doing his famous "Guzzler's Gin" routine and again I sprang my pin. He then introduced his bandleader and vocalist, Ozzie and Harriet Nelson, who did a clever vocal comedic act. When it was finished, Ozzie began his introduction of the next performer and I shall never forget it. Oh, I may not have the words exact, but the context shall echo in my brain forever.

"Friends," he said. "I want to introduce a young comedian who many of you may not know. In fact, it was my two sons Ricky and David who got me listening to his radio show last year. He is delightful and I'd like you to meet that new comedian from Canada — Alan Young."

True Hollywood stars are generous and kind, especially to their own, and the audience broke into immediate response with a lovely wave of applause. I was in shock. I managed to get to my feet and peer from behind the pole. They all laughed, and their applause gave an even kinder welcome. "Oh God," I thought, and it wasn't blasphemy, it was a prayer. "I'm on."

I started down the aisle and, as I felt my waistband slip, I quickly clutched my back. I saw the front of my jacket begin to sway in the breeze so I leaned backwards. This made my view of the stage slightly obscured and I seemed to veer. Instantly one of the waiters, who had been there when I arrived, grasped me firmly and, patting me on the back, confided to a nearby table, "He's slightly disabled. I think he's a veteran." This false information evidently sped through the room as, when I began my routine, which was nothing more than a radio "warm-up," it was greeted with uproarious response. I forgot how I finished but I know it was with a sob of relief. The applause was kind, respectful, and lasted just long enough for me to reach my table. I truly forget the rest of the evening as I spent it securely concealed behind my pole.

When I felt it safe to emerge, I came out and found only the lonely and intoxicated guests slowly preparing to leave. And it was then I witnessed one of the famous lines in Hollywood history.

Louella Parsons, slightly under the influence, was staring at her husband, who was under the coffee table. I recognized him as the physician who had the care of my studio, Twentieth Century-Fox, under his medical wing. Louella was looking around helplessly and finally she gave out the now celebrated statement. "Please help me get 'Docky' up. He's due in surgery in the morning!

Singing with Dorothy Lamour. William Powell thinks somebody's flat! Guess who!

CHAPTER FOUR
HOLLYWOOD HOTCHPOTCH

EXTRAS

Ernie Waggle had appeared in more than 1,600 motion pictures, yet his name was not as well known as Ivor Grench or Caspar Huntoon. Of course, they were two of the top extras in the picture business. Oh, you must have seen them. Naturally, they were always out of focus, but you saw them.

This anonymity suited Ernie just fine. He had long ago forgotten thoughts of riches and stardom. He was content as an extra. But even this meager identification was being lost as, more and more, the extras were being referred to as simply "atmosphere" or "background."

"Is that a movie star?" visitors would ask, looking at Ernie with wide-eyed awe.

"No," the guide would reply. "He's just atmosphere."

Ernie was used to it. It was his lot and that was that. He would never respond to the cheers of stardom, but the director's call of "atmosphere" brought him running.

Extras are called into the set before anyone else. They stand waiting while the stars are primped, polished and photographed. Then they must fade silently into the shadows, waiting patiently for the next urgent call for "atmosphere."

On this particular day, as Ernie slowly wheeled his way through the creeping early morning traffic, he had plenty of time to think, and it was all on the same subject — his future.

He had started out working as an extra in high school pictures, then college and football movies became the rage. In a few years he graduated to army epics and there's where the good money was. In action pictures, an extra can get "bumped" from his basic daily rate of sixty-five dollars up to a few hundred if he manages to get into the action. Handling firearms, being near explosives, working with horses, all brought with them an extra bonus as "hazard" pay.

After a few years, Ernie found he was no longer being called for battle scenes and Western chases. Now in his mid-forties, he was being cast as "atmosphere" for seated audiences, milling crowds and street background. He hadn't had a bump in weeks, and without those bonuses, the extra's income wasn't enough for one to live on let alone a man with a wife and three children.

This day was the closest thing to an action call he'd had in two months. It was only a Western street scene but there were horses to ride, probably some gunplay and maybe a fall or two. Could work out nicely if he got the breaks.

Right after lunch it happened. A scene was to be shot with a runaway stagecoach. A stunt driver was handling the reins, but the director decided it would look more complete with a rider next to him.

"Please give it to me, Harry," Ernie begged the assistant director. "There's nothing to this and I need the money."

The assistant looked doubtful. "I don't know," he said. "It'll be pretty rough up top there."

"Oh, I've done tougher things than that, Harry," Ernie pleaded. "Lemme do it. It'll really help me this week. I've got some extra school bills to pay."

The assistant agreed and Ernie was up on the coach and into position before Harry could give it a second thought or change his mind.

"All right, atmosphere!" called the assistant. "Let's get moving."

"That's not me this time!" thought Ernie happily. "I'm featured in this shot. And a runaway in this rig oughta really be worth something!"

"Take the coach up around the bend," the director said to the driver. "And when I yell for action, I want you to give it to me. Wheel that thing into town like a rocket. Let's go!"

Who knows how the axle broke? A faulty connection, wheel hit a rock? At top speed, it was hard to tell what flipped the coach upside down. The director couldn't explain it. The driver didn't know what happened. Maybe Ernie knew, but he couldn't tell them. He was killed the instant the wagon landed on him. The first thing Ernie saw when he recovered consciousness was this huge shiny gate opening for him as he walked along the cloudy pathway.

"Hello, Ernest," said the kindly gentleman with the beard. "We've been expecting you. In fact, we've got your place all ready."

"I hope I didn't keep you waiting, sir," Ernie said. "What is it you want me to do?"

"Oh, we haven't minded waiting, and there's certainly no rush," laughed the kindly stranger. "This will be your work for all eternity. As long as there are stars in the heavens."

"You mean I finally made the Big Time?" Ernie asked hopefully. "I'm finally going to know what it's like to be a star?"

The man hesitated a second as he saw Ernie's excitement. "No, no, not exactly," he said gently. "We have many bright and powerful stars up here, Gabriel, Michael and all the Arch Angels. But every star must have a setting. You will take your place next to them and serve as sort of an eternal . . . er . . ."

"Atmosphere?" suggested Ernie softly.

"Yes, that's it," the man smiled. "Atmosphere!"

AGENTS

To be a successful performer in Hollywood, one must have talent, training, timing, drive, fortitude, patience and, of course, the most important element of all — an agent.

"But, how do you get an agent?" the actor asks.

Ah, for that you must have talent, training, timing, drive,

fortitude, patience and, of course, the most important element of all — luck.

In the late forties, I decided to drop my agent and get a new one. Being young, and already having a radio show, plus a motion picture contract, it wasn't difficult to find agents who wanted to handle me. But to find the one who would be honest, faithful and give me full attention was another story. Most agents like to have a healthy roster of clients so they can throw the list at a prospective buyer with the idea that "If you don't like this one, how about that one? I've got a million of 'em!" A little like a supermarket. In other words, "A sale is a sale is a sale."

At that time, I was a peripheral Christian Scientist and figured that a quick prayer and good intuition would get me anything. It was called "praying by the seat of your pants."

I went to interview one of Hollywood's top agents who at that time was handling Bob Hope, so I figured he had good connections and as long as his main client had more work than he could handle, the agent would have lots of time for me.

As I sat in his office waiting for him, I looked around at a typical successful agent's surroundings. Expensive furniture, objects d'art and, what was that sitting on the corner of his desk? Why, it's a copy of the Christian Science textbook, *Science and Health with Key to the Scriptures* by Mary Baker Eddy! Wow, do I have intuition or what? At that point the agent came in. "Sorry to keep you waiting," he said, taking a seat behind the desk. "Now, I'm sure you want me to tell you a little about myself."

"You don't need to," I said, smilingly confidentially. "I think I just found out as much about you as I need. Just hand me a contract."

He looked puzzled but shrugged and handed me the papers. I signed, left, and that was that. I don't remember ever hearing from him again. Not only did I not get any work, but I lost one of the jobs I already had! I remember phoning him for advice and he sent an assistant over who got lost trying to find my house. Thank God for the Screen Actors Guild because if, after six months, you don't want to renew an agent, they declare the pact null and void. I was rejoicing in this freedom when I met a beautiful young actress who was just starting in the business. She was also a Christian Scientist and when she heard I was again looking for a new agent she said, "Well, I can tell you this — don't ever sign with '. . .'"

It was the very man I had just dropped. "Oh, I won't," I agreed. I then added, "Tell me, why not?"

"I went to his office about six months ago," she said. "Immediately he began looking me up and down and making very suggestive statements. Then he hit on me."

"He what?" I asked.

"He moved in on me and started groping. I ducked around his desk and he followed. Finally, I was literally running around his office and he was after me. Then I thought, 'Look, you're a Christian Scientist. You can't run out of this office without leaving some kind of blessing.' I remembered I had a paperback copy of Mrs. Eddy's *Science and Health* in my purse. I took it out, dropped it on the corner of his desk and left!"

I suddenly remembered that upon entering this agent's building I saw a girl leaving his office in a bit of a hurry. Evidently I had been his next appointment.

The moral of the story is: To get an agent takes talent, training, timing, drive, fortitude, patience and, above all, forget intuition! Also — "Never judge a booker by his cover."

A LITTLE MORE ABOUT AGENTS

In 1947, my back was broken in a car accident. As I lay in bed at the Hollywood Presbyterian Hospital waiting for my full-body plaster cast to harden, I received a call from my doctor, Zoltan P. Wirtschaffter. (How can I ever forget that name?)

Zoltan was extremely interested in everything about the motion picture business. This was not because he wanted to be a part of it, but as he was not only an internist but also a psychologist, he never ceased to amaze at the patient oxymorons he was meeting in this land of dreams.

I never asked him where he felt I fit in and he kindly never mentioned it. Anyway, he said to me, "Alan, what does an agent do?"

A posed picture. Wouldn't you think they'd connect the phone?

"He gets you work," I answered.

"Does he care what happens to you?"

"He should."

"Yours doesn't."

I paused a moment. "Doctor," I said, "I'm lying here in bed with a vacuum tube blowing hot air on my plaster cast, which is slowly hardening and becoming extremely uncomfortable, not to say painful. I'd love to answer your show business questions, but some other time."

"There's a point to this, Alan," he said. "Your agent just called me and said Fox has picked up your option for a second picture."

"Hmmm," I said. "I wonder why he called you and not me."

"Well, he said the picture goes next week and he wanted to know if you could ride a horse. I said you've got a cast from your neck to your thighs and the ride would kill you. Then he said, 'How about if they make a long shirt so the cast won't show?' I told him that it might stop the cast from showing, but would also stop you from living."

"What did he say to that?" I asked.

"He said he'd get back to me. He seemed to be working on another idea."

I didn't make the picture and six months later I got out of the cast. I also got out of my agency contract.

CHAPTER FIVE
WATCH THEM — THEY'RE TEACHING YOU

Years ago there was a method of teaching children how to swim by simply throwing them in the water. If they made it to the shore, they had learned! If they began to drown, then the father would pull them out and start again. Many of us learned acting the same way.

In other words we were literally thrown on a stage and had to perform our way off. I started at six, playing the part of a clown in a school play, and just never stopped. At thirteen I got my first professional job and stopped doing school plays. If they didn't pay, no play.

Having to scrounge a living by performing didn't leave any time for joining acting classes, and later in my career, I realized that certain techniques were missing from my repertoire, so I began to carefully watch the older, more experienced actors and performers.

I was booked on my first vaudeville job on a New Year's Eve at the Orpheum Theater in Vancouver, British Columbia. It was a rowdy, somewhat boozed crowd, and they greeted each act with what seemed to be organized resentment. Standing backstage with me was an old English music hall performer, who turned to me and said, "You've got to work with a cane."

"Well, I just do impersonations and jokes," I answered.

"You should always work with a cane," he repeated. "You see, if you have a cane when they throw things you just bat it back at them." He demonstrated with a swing that would have done

Hank Aaron proud. "That is unless they throw vegetables. Those you gather up and take home."

It was about this time that I decided radio would be a more sensible way of making a living.

PETER LORRE

In the late fifties I was hired for a supporting role in a TV dramatic series called *Five Fingers*. I was playing a cockney crook and my cohort was that all-time champion miscreant, Peter Lorre. It seemed as if I had seen Peter in movies forever, always playing the sniveling, sneaky character, never realizing that he had been one of Europe's top dramatic actors in his youth. Only in Hollywood was he typecast as the perennial villain.

Being supporting actors, we had a great deal of time between scenes and became quite friendly. I told him I had never had formal acting lessons and he said, "Have you ever worked 'eye-contact' exercises?"

I told him that my only expertise was comedic "takes," "double-takes" and "skulls," so he agreed that we should share our abilities. What he got out of my demonstrations I don't know, but his tutoring was superb.

His eyes were huge and deep but when he fixed them on you it was mesmerizing. I don't know how many muscles the eye has but I'm sure he had a few added when he was in Vienna. No matter how he held his head, those optics bored into you, and no matter how you turned away, your gaze was invariably drawn back.

Finally, Peter was called to work and I had another opportunity to learn some more tricks of our trade. We were shooting in the magnificent Bel Air Hotel and Peter's scene took place in the dining room. He had a long monologue to deliver while eating a plate of caviar. He rehearsed with the real stuff and his unctuous dialogue was only surpassed by his licentious, almost sensual enjoyment of the caviar.

The time came to shoot and oddly, though he had it letter-perfect in rehearsal, Peter kept forgetting the lines. He didn't seem upset about this, even when they had done over five takes. When they finished shooting, I said, "Peter, you knew the lines perfectly. What happened?"

He grinned mischievously. "I just couldn't bear to have the scene end. I mean, that was imported caviar. The best I've had in years!"

CLIFTON WEBB

He had received accolades and an Oscar nomination for his work in *Laura* (1944), and then became a major star with *Sitting Pretty* (1948), but he still had to fulfill his contract with Twentieth Century-Fox, so he was cast as Shirley Temple's co-star in a sequel called *Mr. Belvedere Goes to College* (1949).

I was playing my usual part of a nerd. The leading man was a stiff, self-centered young man whom Clifton spotted immediately as such. During the first scene, when the young actor attempted to establish his method of acting, which ignored his fellow performers, Clifton turned on him with all the rightful venom his station demanded. I would have died. This young man simply withered, but that was enough to clear the decks.

On my first scene with Webb I was petrified. I had been a star of radio from the age of sixteen, but this was the movies. After the rehearsal, I got up enough nerve to speak to him personally. "Mr. Webb," I said, "I hope I'm giving you what you want. If not, please tell me."

He stared at me coldly. "Are you putting me on, young man?" he responded.

"No, no," I said. "I love comedy, and unless you get a proper feed, it's hard to respond."

He smiled. "Thank you," he said. "So I'll tell you something. I'm standing in your key light. Do you know what that means?"

Here I am back in college with Clifton Webb.

I shrugged ignorantly and so he showed me. He stepped back slightly and I felt visible. "I don't know anything about the picture business," I confessed.

"That," he sniffed, "you are making painfully evident." Then he smiled. "So keep your eye on me, young man. To begin with, make sure nobody stands in your key light. It's like being upstaged in the theater." From then on we got along beautifully. I supported him and I'll never forget how he saved me.

I had been doing the Jimmy Durante radio show in the evening while working all day in the picture. After the radio broadcast I rushed home because I had to get up the next day for filming. As I walked through my door the lights went on and there was the whole Durante cast, with Jimmy at the piano, singing "Happy Birthday." I had forgotten what day it was. With Jimmy there, it was a fabulous evening and, finally, at about eleven, he began to play his famous "Goodnight, goodnight" number, which heralded their exit. In the excitement, I had forgotten to look at my next

Rehearsing with Jimmy Durante on his radio show.

day's shooting schedule. It was my big scene and I had two pages
of dialogue to learn, then get up at 5:00 A.M.!

With many actors, the more pressure, the less memory, and that
was certainly true with me. I arrived at the studio still mumbling
the lines and they weren't coming easily. The scene wasn't
shot until late in the afternoon, but that didn't help. I was not
prepared. To make matters worse, the scene was between Clifton
and me, with me doing most of the talking.

We began rehearsing. I flubbed and forgot. "Don't worry,
young man," Clifton said kindly. "It's just a rehearsal. It'll all
flood back."

It didn't. The more blanks I drew, the more came up. We had
reached take seven and I had reached quiet hysteria. Finally,
Clifton spoke up to the director. "Elliott," he said, "it's four thirty
and I'm tired. Frankly I don't feel I'm giving Alan the motivation
he needs. Can we shut down and start in the morning?"

Of course they obeyed. You can't argue with a star, and right
then he was one of the greatest stars in my heaven!

Howard Hughes

Many stories have been written about this eccentric man, but one thing is certain: His father left him four million dollars and he parlayed it into billions. Hardly the accomplishment of a cretin. The money began with the Hughes Tool Company, based in Texas, and resulted from the leasing of a special drilling bit invented by his father. Howard kept this company as the focal point of his endeavors for years. In fact, when I was under contract to him, all my checks came from the tool company! Naturally, I had been told of his eccentricities, but it wasn't until I began work at his studio, RKO, that I saw them first-hand.

Dear Jane was inviting me to sit down — somewhere else!

A huge cast had been hired for his picture *Androcles and the Lion* (1952). Many of the actors had been brought especially from England. After three days shooting, we were all told to go home and take two weeks off. The salary continued, of course, so none of us minded too much. In fact, it was a good laugh when we found the reason.

Some ten years before Hughes had produced a picture called *The Outlaw*, starring his newest find, Jane Russell. Most of the film was directed by Howard Hawks, and when he quit, Hughes took up the reins. He shot some scenes of the generously and beautifully endowed Miss Russell, which the powerful Hays Office objected to. Hughes would not cut the scenes and the Hays Office remained adamant, so the picture stayed on the shelf. Jane continued to receive top publicity coverage for years, even though she had never been seen! Howard continued to be completely inflexible, spending millions on promoting both Jane and the picture. In those days, the large studios also owned chains of theaters throughout the land, so Howard's picture couldn't have found an outlet even if the Hays Office had relented.

About 1950, he discovered that the RKO studios were in a financial position that suggested they could be bought for a price, and he had the cash. He didn't particularly want the studio, but they owned innumerable top theaters in major cities. Finally, after ten years he could have a place to release his picture!

He hired top publicists to build the biggest promotional campaign the motion picture business had ever seen — and we now learned the reason for our two-week vacation. Every carpenter, grip and artisan in the studio was called away from whatever they were doing and put on Howard's "special project." After two weeks, when we all reported back to work, we saw the result of their work.

They had been constructing a huge billboard with an ornate plaster frame in the center of which was a gigantic picture of Jane in the pose the Hays Office had fought against so valiantly. It took house-moving equipment to transport it down to Wilshire Boulevard, where it was to stand three stories high, for all to see.

We had barely returned to work when again there was a delightful hiatus. The details of this were later related to me by Gower Champion, who was staging the dance numbers for an RKO musical. He had completed the choreography on the finale and wanted Howard Hughes to see it and give his okay. He put a call into the production office to say he had everything ready

Jane Russell ignoring me completely again.

for Mr. Hughes' inspection. In a matter of minutes he received an order: "Bring it over." Hughes operated from an office he rented from Sam Goldwyn studios and had only been on his own lot once — when he bought it.

Gower protested to Johnny Meyers, Hughes' right-hand man, that the dance number involved intricate moves around the huge set, which had built-in props. Meyer's response was, "Mr. Hughes says, 'Bring it over.'"

It took the whole day to dismantle the set and load it onto trucks. The next day the set was transported to the Sam Goldwyn studio six blocks away! There it was unloaded and set up on a soundstage. This took another day. Gower and the dancers came in on the third day and Howard was told that everything was ready. He came down from his office and watched the number. It took ten minutes. He nodded his approval and went back to his office. Two more days were spent in dismantling, transporting and resetting at RKO, then we could all get back to work.

Howard Hughes' romances were legend and mostly apocryphal. He had an eye and liking for beauty but as he was shy and discriminating, there was very little follow-through.

One day, Jeanne Mahoney, a pretty young girl who danced on my show, came to visit me on the set. Hughes must have had spies in every corner because within hours she was asked to pose for a picture which was to be sent to Mr. Hughes. Shortly after that, she was given a six-month contract and told that there was an apartment waiting for her on Pico Boulevard, as she was now the property of RKO. Her brother, Tommy, found everything was on the up and up, so she moved in. Nobody from the studio bothered her and she never met her boss Howard. When the contract was up, she returned home and went back to work dancing on my show. It was found later that Howard had apartments all over Los Angeles where pretty young actresses were housed, protected and puzzled.

Audrey Totter, a lovely and talented actress of the early 1950s, told me her experience, which I think captures the convoluted character of Howard Hughes. She was introduced to him and immediately he asked her if she would go with him for dinner, dancing and whatever. She liked the dinner and dancing, but the "whatever" gave her pause. However, she thought, "Why not?" She was a big girl and could take care of herself. She bought a beautiful dress for the occasion, had her hair done at the studio, and that evening Howard picked her up.

They had a delightful dinner at one of L.A.'s finest restaurants and she said he was a perfect gentleman and thoughtful host. They didn't dance, and, for a while, she wondered if he was skipping that part and heading straight for the "whatever." Near the end of the dinner, he was called to the telephone, and when he returned, he said that they would have to rush over to his hanger because the engineers were having trouble with his *Spruce Goose*.

"A-ha," she thought. "Here it comes."

Now, Audrey hadn't just fallen off the watermelon truck, but this was the newest, most innovative line she had ever heard, so she said she just had to go with him, even if it meant a full-length view of his *Spruce Goose*, whatever the hell that was! She was amazed when he drove over to Hughes Aircraft on Imperial Highway, where they entered a hanger and here was the biggest wooden airplane she had ever seen. She climbed up a ladder, evening dress and all, and went inside with him. He got a chair for her and said he wouldn't be long, then went into the cockpit with a couple of engineers.

Ten minutes later he came back, his smart blue suit covered in oil, and was most apologetic. The engine problem was a big one and would take him the rest of the night. But he'd called for a car to take her home. He went back to the cockpit, she got into the limo, went home and she never saw him again.

Some time later her mother became quite ill and it was decided that the only proper treatment she could get was at a famous clinic in the east, a very expensive proposition. How Howard ever found out about this, Audrey could never imagine, but within days, word was sent to her that her mother had a free ticket on TWA and all medical expenses were being taken care of by Hughes Tool Company.

Evidently, his concern for friends and employees didn't stop with beautiful ladies. During the time of my RKO contract, it was necessary for me to take a night flight to New York. For some reason, the plane sat on the runway for ten minutes before taking off. Later, my wife phoned me in New York and said that as the plane began to taxi out it suddenly stopped and she saw Howard Hughes hurry over to it and spend the next ten minutes inspecting it from nose to tail.

I understand that when Elizabeth Bergner wanted to fly to New York, he bumped the passengers onto another flight so she could have the plane all to herself. This story I can't vouch for, but all reliable sources indicate its truth.

Couldn't Hollywood do with a few independent characters like this now? These people are marvelous copy, don't hurt anybody, and, perhaps, bring a little courtesy into our world.

CHAPTER SIX
THE GOOD OLD DAYS — OR
"HAVE I BEEN AROUND THAT LONG?"

It could have been Sam Goldwyn who said, "Nostalgia is not what it used to be," but it would seem that the younger audiences, along with the older, have a great appetite for the movies and TV shows of the '50s and '60s. "Must've been fun then," some of them say. "I mean, it didn't seem so frantic."

I'm not too fond of the expressions "The Good Old Days" or "When I was a kid," but I appreciated the essence of the question. They were asking how was it in those days when the pond was peaceful and the country gentle, when the emphasis was on the word "show" not so much on "business."

Oh, I'm sure the moguls then were manipulating, but we didn't mind because their sense of the public was good. They loved making money but their taste and responsibility drew a line, and they appointed their own watchdog to make sure that none of them overstepped the mark. Nobody wanted the government to step in with the dreaded threat of censorship.

I can well remember as a child in Canada attending a movie, and seeing the Canadian Film Board suddenly black out the screen and insert a "Scene Censored" notice. We howled our derision and tried to imagine what filth had been deleted, only to later find it was the delightfully innocent scene in *It Happened One Night* where Clark Gable and Claudette Colbert hung a protective screen between their twin beds! Sometimes "Big Brother" can become too big, and make us more inquisitive.

I have no better answer to give to those young minds enquiring about the "old days" but to simply say, "It was nice."

With the studios demanding a six-day week, and the privilege of working the actors until all hours on Saturdays, there was no time for trips to Vegas. In fact, until the fifties, Las Vegas had only a couple of well-known hotels and was anything but the swinging town it is today.

If one were working, leisure time was spent close to home, as there weren't that many spots to dine or cavort. Actors found themselves spending many off hours in the company of others in the craft. The ones who didn't appreciate this camaraderie generally stayed home or found exclusive out-of-the-way restaurants.

For those who liked to meet each other or be seen, it was Ciro's or the Coconut Grove for dinner and dancing, then off to Charlie Morrison's Mocambo for late snacks, drinks and more dancing. The younger lot generally headed for the Palladium to enjoy the Big Bands like the Dorseys or Harry James. The large show houses like the Florentine Gardens were more for the visiting firemen and tourists. We lunched at the Brown Derby in Hollywood or Beverly Hills and if we had enough money it was a nice Sunday brunch at the Beverly Hills Hotel.

My first introduction to this "family-feel" was a few months after my arrival in town. I had to take skating lessons for a picture called *Margie* (1946), and Fox sent me to Sonja Henie's Ice Rink. There, I found myself skating with a whole group of younger actors and stars: Mickey Rooney, Jane Powell, Elizabeth Taylor, Roddy McDowall, Jeanne Crain and many of the studios' junior stable. I remember taking one look at those almost purple eyes of Elizabeth Taylor's and thinking, "That's the most beautiful little face I've ever seen." Then, when she spoke with an English accent, the ice melted for three feet around me.

It was pleasant to walk down Hollywood Boulevard from my hotel, the Plaza at Vine Street, and gape at the stars strolling by, or cross the street and go to the Hollywood Brown Derby for dinner and see the radio stars having a quick meal between shows.

Tying Jeanne Crain's skates. Wouldn't you?

And have one smile at me and say, "Hey, you're the new kid on the block. Nice show, Alan."

"Thanks, the same to you, Mr. Skelton."

"Mr. Skelton? That's my father's name. I'm Red!"

A lovely old response, but so warm and sincerely delivered. Yes, they were old days, I guess, and they were beautiful.

NBC was on Sunset Boulevard, a block south of the Derby, and CBS was two blocks east. Then NBC had corralled all of the comedy shows, while CBS had the plays and dramatic series, such as *Lux Radio Theater*, with host Cecil B. DeMille, and *Mister District Attorney*, a top-rated crime drama.

In the halcyon days of radio, there were really only two national networks: NBC and CBS. For some reason, by either predicament or plan, NBC was the major comedy network and CBS broadcast radio dramas. Later, NBC was forced to split their system into two — the Red network and the Blue network.

With Van Johnson and Dorothy Lamour on her radio show, around 1948.

My show became a part of the Blue network. We broadcast in the old Fox studios on Sunset Boulevard, which hadn't been used for twenty years. There is nothing more desolate than a deserted motion picture lot with empty, musty soundstages and decaying sets. I was given a dressing room, but wouldn't go near it. I swear one of Bela Lugosi's old jackets was hanging in the closet. Our show tickets had a map printed on the back, but, even then, very few people found the place. They might have even needed passports, I'm not sure. Finally, my sponsor decided to invest another five thousand per week so I could hire "name" guest stars.

Realizing that such great names as Edward G. Robinson, Rita Hayworth, Basil Rathbone, Dame May Whitty, Charles Laughton and many more were going to be on their network, NBC decided it would be more fitting to move me into the more appropriate studios at Hollywood and Vine. I look back at that series of broadcasts with a tinge of regret as I had some of the top stars in the movie business as guests and never thought to have pictures taken. I had hoped my manager, who was also the packager of the show, might have done it, but it would have added another twenty or thirty dollars to the budget and he was so tight, his pores had disappeared. He not only had the first dollar he ever earned but he had the man's right arm that gave it to him. Clear enough picture?

Dinah Shore, my co-star in *Aaron Slick from Punkin Crick*, not one of Paramount's best.

Working at the NBC studios immediately made you a part of a large famous family. It was a "U"-shaped building with the cross portion containing offices and the two legs were hallways having a studio on either side — four in all. At the end of each hallway were ladies and gentlemen's restrooms. I attempt to draw a clear picture of the set-up as it lent itself to a great family cooperative situation.

On my first visit to the men's room, I was washing my hands when in walked Jack Benny. I'd listened to him since I was a kid and here he was relieving himself just like anybody else! And he does it just the way I do, too! I had finished drying my hands when Bob Hope entered. He began talking to Jack and I didn't want to miss a word so I began washing my hands again. As they left, Fibber McGee came in, so for me it was back to the basin. Tuesday was a big broadcast day for the comedians so the restrooms were busy. I had chapped hands for a week, but it was worth it.

The advantage of all the comedy shows being rehearsed and broadcast in the same area was they could assist each other. For example, if at the last minute Bob Hope's writers couldn't come up with a good punch ending for a sketch, he could approach Red Skelton in the hall or dressing room and ask if he would walk on and deliver a finish line as a favor. The audience would scream its approval and the show ended with a bang.

I witnessed the terrific benefit this arrangement had when I was the guest star on Dinah Shore's radio show. Incidentally, the writers of the show were fresh out of college and I think this was their first assignment. Bob Lawrence and Robert Lee would later go on to write many legitimate productions, *Mame* being their greatest success. *The Dinah Shore Show* was a very popular radio program with music and comedy, the *piece de resistance* being a five-minute closing musical arrangement featuring the vocal talents of Dinah. The program went well and as we reached the finale, it looked like a winner — until, in the middle of the vocal, Dinah began to lose her voice. It wasn't too noticeable to the audience, but to us who had been rehearsing all week it was an obvious tragedy. Fortunately all the shows were carried on loudspeakers in the hall, the dressing rooms and even in the restrooms. I don't know where Bing Crosby was when he heard the problem, but, within seconds, our stage door opened and he strode in, joining in on the song, walking to the mike and taking over as a fading Dinah gratefully backed away. Even the studio audience thought it was part of a well-planned production, but we knew it was the members of the show-business family in action.

JIMMY DURANTE

Few people realize that over a 30-year period, Jimmy wrote almost 100 songs, which were used in Broadway shows, records, radio and nightclubs. Then, when he went into TV, he composed as many again. For years, the Jimmy Durante Music Publishing Company on Yucca Street in Hollywood was a familiar tourist attraction. I don't know how much activity the company generated, but it was a place for Jimmy to place many of his old buddies and hangers-on, whom he kept on salary.

Leo Soloman, David R. Schwartz and me — a good writing team!

Visiting the *Variety* offices, which were next door, I bumped into Jimmy, and while talking to him, I noticed three or four of his entourage staring out of the office window. Jimmy finally saw them. "Sorry, Youngie, I got to go," he said. "My Chairman of the Board and the directors want me to buy 'em breakfast."

When I was working on the Durante radio show, we often had script meetings at Jimmy's Beverly Hills home. It was a modest but lovely house on Canon Drive. Jimmy had just built a den in the back patio overlooking the pool, which was his favorite spot, and he was so proud of his newest acquisition, that we held our script rehearsals there.

The decorator had installed beautiful wormy-chestnut paneling. I'd had the same wood put in my den and realized how expensive it was.

"Great bookcase, Jimmy," I said.

"Yeah, but lookit the old wood he used," Jimmy said. "And he ain't painted it yet!"

At the next meeting I noticed that the wormholes had been carefully spackled and the whole bookcase had been painted eggshell-white! I spent a recent New Year's Eve as Margie Durante's guest; the first time I'd been in the house since 1948. The den was the same and the bookcases still pristine Durante-white.

No doubt the following story should be listed under "famous practical jokes" but since the account epitomizes the character of Jimmy Durante, we'll leave it at that. I worked for Jimmy on his radio show from 1948 to the summer of 1949. One of his stooges was Candy Candido, a very funny little man with an unbelievable trick voice.

Each morning Candy would drop by Jimmy's house to drive him to the studio, and he always arrived a little early to make sure they got to the rehearsal on time. Invariably, Jimmy was just beginning his breakfast, a bowl of cornflakes. He always invited Candy to sit down and wait, but never asked him to have any cornflakes with him. So after a few days, Candy began to bring over his own box of flakes as a hint. Jimmy's only comment was

"Didn't ya bring no milk for yerself?"

One morning Jimmy was so furious he could hardly eat his breakfast. "Them boids is messin' up my pool erria," he fumed. "Dey crap everywhere."

The next morning Candy noticed that Jimmy had strung chicken wire over the pool as protection. But all it did was enable the birds to have a place to sit while they hit the pool directly. Jimmy was not furious but helpless. Candy's devious mind went to work and he got an idea that might alleviate the situation. He went to a pet shop and asked if they had any birds.

"Certainly, sir," the owner responded. "What kind of bird?"

"A dead one."

At first, the salesman was taken aback, but then, being used to the cracks and quirks of Hollywood, he rose to the occasion. Yes, a bird had died and Candy could have it at no charge.

The next morning he arrived at Jimmy's a little earlier, sneaked over the back fence and dropped the bird into the pool. Then he went around to the front door and rang the bell. As he and Jimmy

were eating their flakes Jimmy looked out to his patio and gasped. "There's a dead boid swimmin' inna pool!" he exploded.

"I'll take care of it, Jimmy," said Candy. He rushed into the bedroom, and a moment later emerged completely naked except for a pair of shoes. He ran to the edge of the pool and dove in. As he was in the air, he heard Jimmy's voice yelling, "Take yer shoes off foist!"

He retrieved the little body and climbed out of the pool. Jimmy was furious. "Ya shouldnta dove inta the pool wit yer shoes on!"

Candy looked at him innocently. "They're not my shoes, Jim, they're yours."

ED GARDINER

Ed was the star of a popular radio show in the forties called *Duffy's Tavern*. He played the bartender, a rough-talking Brooklynite, which didn't take any acting on Ed's part. That was him.

We had the same sponsor, Bristol-Myers, and when I came west, we shared the same advertising agency, so were thrown together a great deal. As I said, he was a diamond in the rough, the diamond being buried deeply in a lot of rough. However, like most men of his type, he was gentle and kind to the babes in the wood. I was not exactly a babe, but I was lost in the woods of agency machinations, and he knew it.

One day I went to the men's room at NBC and there sat Ed, relieving himself in one of the cubicles. He never bothered shutting the door and when I entered he greeted me warmly. "Hey, Alan," he said. "I hear yer havin' problems wit the advertisin' agency."

"Yes," I answered sadly. "They want me to put things into the show that are just not practical."

He let out a straining grunt as he continued his business. I wanted to leave him to his exertion but it seemed a mite rude.

"The trouble with them is," he paused to grunt a little more pressure, "they don't know nuthin' [grunt], and people like me and an' you who have a sense of decency get pushed around [grunt]. The trouble with the whole bunch of agency people is [grunt] they're just plain crude!"

———◆———

The first "Miss Duffy" on Ed's show was played by his then-wife Shirley Booth, one of New York's great actresses. When they were first married, Ed was the manager of a theatrical group of which

Shirley was the star. She used to recount this story herself.

They were previewing their play in a New England town, prior to the New York opening. After the performance, they returned to their hotel, went to bed and started making love. Things were progressing beautifully when there was a knock at the door. Ed immediately stopped all activity, left Shirley lying there, slipped on a robe and answered the door.

It was the unit manager asking about the next day's rehearsal plans. Ed discussed the matter with him at some length. After five or ten minutes they concluded their business. Ed shut the door, removed his robe, got into bed and turned to Shirley. "Now, where wuz we?" he asked.

Harry Cohn

One of the unquestioned despots of the motion picture business was Harry Cohn, the head of Columbia Studios. Stories of his idiosyncrasies and inclemency were Hollywood fodder for years. He was indisputably a great and successful producer, but his methods of achieving this reputation were appalling. Absolutely nothing stood in his way of getting what he wanted.

I never met Mr. Cohn, but my one encounter with him is quite vivid in memory. I was performing in a benefit show at Ciro's and just before going on stage someone said excitedly, "Harry Cohn has just arrived!"

My heart jumped into my throat and I swallowed it back down. "Where's he sitting?" I asked.

"He's not. He's standing in the doorway at the back of the hall. Probably can't stay long."

I was introduced and went on. Uppermost in my thought was the fact that I hoped my performance wasn't the one that made Mr. Cohn decide to leave. As I got my first laugh, it was an opportunity to look around the audience. I spotted him standing in the doorway, surrounded by what appeared to be his lackeys and the one standing at Mr. Cohn's shoulder seemed to be enjoying my performance.

Suddenly, I was auditioning, but no matter what material I used, the cigar never left Mr. Cohn's mouth. He just stared. Finally, I used one of my sure-fire bits. The man at Harry's shoulder laughed appreciatively and with that Harry took the cigar out of his mouth, and turned to his friend, not realizing that he was holding the cigar at face level. He got his associate right in the eye.

As I went on with my act, I could see his friend gesturing that it was nothing at all. Meanwhile, his eye was shut and tears were streaming down his cheek. They continued to watch the show with Harry puffing and his lackey wiping his eye. I finished quickly and left, hoping never to have to work for Columbia Pictures. There was nothing to worry about on that score as I got the impression that Mr. Cohn felt the same way about me.

Harry's longtime secretary was a sweet young thing named Virginia Smith. Of course, she has since retired, but I see her from time to time. One day Harry was fuming as one of the actresses he had built to stardom had the effrontery to turn down a role he had picked for her.

"I don't need her," roared Harry. "I made her a star and I can make any girl a star. I'll give this part to the next girl who walks past that window."

In a moment or two, a girl walked by and Harry immediately called her in.

Her name was "Marilyn Pauline . . ."

"We can't use that name," Harry said. Then he turned to his little secretary. "What'll we call her, Virginia?"

Virginia smiled sweetly as she thought, and then finally answered. "What about Kim Novak?"

One more Harry Cohn story. While this one seems apocryphal, it's worth repeating. However, it could very well be true. As I said, his underlings were always nervous when he was around, particularly the office staff, who were all candidates for early ulcers. That is, all but one man who went through the day perpetually happy and seemingly carefree. No matter what the Cohn cyclones, this man remained serene.

Finally they simply had to discover his secret. They knew the man was a Christian Scientist, and they noticed that each morning when he arrived, he went directly into his office, shut the door and didn't come out for five or ten minutes. When he emerged, his face was smiling and peaceful.

One morning after he entered his office and shut the door, one of the staff quietly took a chair over to the transom above his door and peered in. The man was sitting in his chair, hands folded, eyes shut and was repeating over and over, "There is no Harry Cohn, there is no Harry Cohn, there is no Harry Cohn!"

JOHN WAYNE

In criticizing an actor for a dubious performance, a newspaper critic once wrote, "He must have taken acting lessons from John Wayne." Well, that may have been a slam at both of them, but I'm free to admit that I took an acting lesson from John Wayne.

It happened when I was living near him in Newport Beach. The Wayne home was on a promontory of land in an exclusive section known as Bayshores. It was a fine but not particularly palatial residence, typical of the man. Moored on his private dock was his yacht, *Wild Goose*. This was his compact Shangri-la, where weekends were enjoyed away from his constantly active productions.

Saturday evenings were movie nights, when the studio would send down a projectionist with the latest unreleased feature. A small coterie of friends was invited to the viewing and, through Wayne's gracious wife Pilar, a mutual friend included me in the permanent invitation.

Generally, the pictures were ones that John would enjoy, as his taste was quite eclectic. But now and again a dud or avant-garde film would appear and, at such times, he would quietly slip out of the viewing room to have a drink and schmooze with a friend or two. Or have a drink or two and schmooze with a friend. John was flexible.

One Saturday, Ibsen's *The Seagull* came on the screen. The music was dirge-like, the photography extremely diffused and "arty" and the movement slow. Wayne fidgeted. He nudged me and we both took off for the den.

"Hell," he snorted when we got there, "I've got those damn birds crapping all over my boat. I don't wanna see a movie about them!"

Then came my acting lesson. "Alan," he said, "I started to talk slow and leave lotsa . . . spaces in my speech . . . because I figured the . . . longer it took me ta . . . get the line finished, the . . . longer the camera would hafta . . . stay on me."

He then told me how he handled so-called Method actors. In an early picture, he had a scene with a young actor who made it clear to everyone that his main love was the "real" art of the theater and he was simply giving Hollywood a whirl. John stood patiently while the actor performed his "get in the mood" gyrations, and the rehearsal started. The actor had only one line to say and then he had to listen to John's speech. While John was talking, the young man took a cigarette out, lit it, took a long drag, then exhaled slowly. John continued his speech, seemingly oblivious to anything else, but before the actual take, he took the actor aside.

"What is that you did in rehearsal with the cigarette?" he asked pleasantly.

"Oh that," the young man lightly replied. "That's just my little piece of business."

John smiled then said, quietly, "You do that during the shot and I'm gonna ram my knee into your other little piece of business — if you've got one!"

It became a nonsmoking scene.

STAN LAUREL

I received a call from Dr. Alexander Stern, our family doctor, who lived on our street in North Hollywood. He invited me for dinner saying he had a friend who wanted to meet me. At that time, I was doing a live TV revue, which had been well received, and, for a time, I was a guest on many dinner lists, so I took this date as a favor to our doctor. Little did I know . . .

On entering the apartment I saw a beaming face which I had seen and almost worshiped for years.

"Here's the man who's been wanting to meet you, Alan," said my host. "Meet Mr. Stan Laurel."

Stan Laurel, the most humble and gentle star I've ever known.

I could hardly talk. I think I managed to get out an "oh, oh!" or some such abstruse statement.

"Ee, I've wanted to meet you, son," Stan said in an English north-country accent I instantly recognized. "You do the kind of comedy I love."

He then brought out a large white book and asked if I would autograph it for him. It was his membership book in an old London theatrical club called "The Water Rats," and he had the signatures of famous performers down through the years. How I ever signed it with my hand shaking so much, I'll never imagine.

Later in the evening, we discovered that our families had lived near each other in the town of Shields in Northumberland. In fact, as children, my father and aunt had run away from home to audition for Stan's father, a Glasgow impresario whom I had always heard referred to as Mr. Jefferson, Stan's real last name. I'm grateful they weren't hired, as by now I'd probably be a music hall comic or still a gleam in some bagpipe player's eye.

We had a couple of other dates together, but each time, I just sat and stared in frozen admiration at this humble, sweet little man. After he passed away, I realized that I had never asked for his autograph, and he had mine! However, about ten years ago, a woman came up to me at a party and introduced herself as Lois Laurel, Stan's daughter. She gave me a picture of herself with her Dad and on it she wrote: "My father always said that you were a very funny young man."

I finally got my picture of him! True, it's signed by his daughter but somehow I feel he had a hand in it.

With Hal Roach, famous silent comedy producer, and creator of *Our Gang* comedies. Hal talked to me about remaking some of his old shorts. It would have been great to have worked with this comedy master.

Whoever referred to the early days of live television as "The Golden Days" was obviously never a part of it. It may have been golden in the eyes of the viewer, but it was lead in the stomach of the performer. There was no videotape, no retakes, generally one quick camera rehearsal and you were on. Bobble a line and it bounced from coast-to-coast. Forget a line and you'd better have something fascinating to say because millions of eyes were staring. Conversations the day after a big show were interesting:

Early TV — *The Alan Young Show,* 1950.

"Did you see the Young show last night where the chair accidentally broke as he sat down?"

"Yeah, I thought his ad lib was pretty good: 'I knew I'd get it in the end.'"

"Oh, that's all planned. The writers give him that ahead of time."

I'd like to show him the planned lump on my coccyx, and while he's down there he can kiss it.

Even underwater I didn't know how to handle women.

My CBS show was broadcast from Studio "A," in what is now KCBS radio in Hollywood. It was a perfect studio for radio broadcasts, in fact Cecil B. DeMille's *Lux Radio Theater* came from there as did the Armed Forces Broadcasts and other major productions. The studio held a little over two hundred people, which was just right for intimate rapport with the audience. There was a camera island in the middle of the audience, about three feet over their heads, and a camera was on islands on each side of the studio.

How can I be here — and there?

In the middle of one of the broadcasts, I caught a flash of something flying over the heads of the audience. Naturally, the theater was dark, but out of the corner of my eye I could see this activity. It was also obvious that the audience was fascinated by this unexpected action as we were getting applause in very odd places.

I could hardly wait for the show to finish so I could rush over to the director and ask what had been going on. It seems that in the middle of our first sketch, the number one camera reported a lens malfunction. Quickly, the director checked the upcoming shots and relayed them to the cameramen. They would then remove their own lens after using it, and toss it over the audience to the camera with the shot coming up. The audience had been following this drama with great interest and to the exclusion of whatever had been taking place on stage. The applause came

Oh, I get it. It's a Kinescope!

when one of the cameramen made a difficult and spectacular
catch! Golden Days?

On hot summer days, the stage would become oppressive and
so the side scenery doors would be left open for ventilation, even
during a broadcast. The set construction building was across the
street and many times I've been in the middle of a sketch and
glanced offstage to see the stage-hands rushing the flats across
the parking lot and into the theater. There they would be erected
just in time for the second sketch. I never liked this because the
paint was always still wet and if you accidentally touched or
brushed up against the flat, you walked around for the rest of the
scene trying to keep your painted side away from the camera!

It was always a thrill to have old pros come on the show and,
even though they had never performed in television, they had been
through the theatrical mill long enough to adapt to anything.
James Gleason, the famous fight manager in the great movie
Here Comes Mr. Jordan, made his TV debut on my show and
part of his job was to introduce the sketch. He spoke in front of

a small flat, which was used to conceal the set behind him. As he finished his comedy introduction he turned upstage, the flat was whisked away and he entered the scene.

In rehearsal it worked beautifully but during the show, the heat from the stage lights, plus the presence of an audience, made the backstage atmosphere unbearable, so, as usual, someone opened the scene doors. This caused a gentle breeze, which evidently blew directly onto the flat behind Jimmy. The flats were made of light pine and canvas to ensure quick and easy removal. They also have the properties of a jib sail and are quick to respond to the slightest breath of wind. As I was standing in the wings awaiting my entrance, I witnessed the whole adventure. As the camera was shooting straight on, the activity was almost unnoticeable to the viewer, but the studio audience and I had a great time.

The flat gently tipped over and leaned against Jimmy's head. He quickly realized what had happened and, without a break in his dialogue, he made a quick head gesture to push the flat back in place. It responded immediately, but then reacted even more quickly to another gust of wind and returned strongly, this time hitting the brim of his hat, which made it lift off his head in a mysterious effect. The audience was now aware of the predicament and, being familiar with the vagaries of live television, was enjoying it to the full. I sometimes think that was their main reason for attending live shows, a little like the citizens of Rome watching the Christians fight lions.

Jimmy was now halfway through his monologue and you could see that all of his artistic adrenaline was flowing full force. He was ready, not welcoming, any further developments. The monologue, which was scheduled for around forty seconds, had now stretched into over two minutes with no immediate end in sight. The offending stage door had been shut, but the flat was now completely free of its moorings and was resting affectionately on Jimmy's shoulders.

With great timing, he dramatically spun away from the errant piece of scenery, giving a waiting stagehand a chance to grab it off-camera, and then made a triumphant entrance into the sketch.

Ground-breaking for the Encino Theatre, circa 1952, with Duncan Renaldo ("The Cisco Kid") and an unknown woman — I wish I'd known!!

I had never seen the introduction to a scene get what amounted to a near standing ovation!

Continuing the saga of these great unsung old troupers, one of our regulars was a little man whose face was instantly recognizable from the many movies he had appeared in. Sometimes Chester Clute was the meek husband, or the beleaguered bank clerk, or an innocent victim. His roles were never large, but his laughs were. He was what was euphemistically and gratefully called "a scene saver."

The first time we cast him, he played the part of a meek husband who was purchasing a boat he didn't want, but his socially

With Charles Coburn on *The Alan Young Show*.

ambitious wife was in charge. As I have said, our sets were erected
hurriedly, not because the builders were incapable, far from it.
But we generally got the script finished at the last minute and
the poor designer and carpenters had to work overtime. In this
instance they worked overtime and built a fine boat set, but
again, the paint wasn't dry and a few other things had been
hurriedly completed.

As a boat salesman, I was showing Chester around the yacht.
I saw that he had leaned against some wet paint and now his
white jacket-sleeve was sporting a distinct mahogany smudge.
He noticed it too, so from then on we adjusted our staging so
that his offending arm was up stage, away from the camera.

Believe it or not, that's the unemotional Nelson Eddy!

Next, he put his head out one of the portholes to see the view and, as fate and a hurried carpenter would have it, a nail was sticking out, so when he drew his head back out of the porthole, the nail gashed the side of his cheek, not badly, but enough to draw blood. He now had to hold his hand over his left cheek and keep it away from the camera, while also keeping his right side out of view. Being in the scene, I couldn't tell him that the camera would focus on me and he needn't worry, but it was great watching this gutsy little guy carry on. The rest of his performance resembled a contortionist trying to escape from his jacket and when we were off the air, the audience, the band, and the cast gave him an ovation.

Later, with tears in his eyes, he told me that it was the first time in his long career that he had ever starred! Chester is gone now, but I'm sure he wouldn't mind my telling this final story about him. He loved working on the show and was always reliable, no matter what he had to do.

I have the feeling my wife is attracted to Cesar Romero.

One day I saw him standing backstage and told him that we had a dressing room for him to rest in.

"Oh no," he said. "I never tire of being backstage and watching the activity. It's life to me."

I discovered later that his wife had recently passed away and he missed her, but being on the show had given him a fresh enthusiasm. From then on, we used him fairly regularly, even on the commercials, which we shot after the show went off the air. It was then we found little Chester's one tiny secret. He would retire to his dressing room after the performance and while taking his makeup off, he'd sip the contents of a small flask he'd brought, obviously filled with his favorite nectar. Then, refreshed and slightly heady, this reborn little performer would wend his way back to his hotel, alone but happy.

One of my guests on *The Alan Young Show*, 1951, Ilene Woods, who had recently completed her voice-over role as Cinderella in the Disney classic.

After one show, we shot a commercial, using Chester in it, and then wrapped for the night. Chester went off to his room and as I was changing, I received word from the producer that the control room reported a problem with the kinescope machine. Before tape, the only way to record a TV show was to place a kinescope camera in front of the bare TV tube and record the picture. It was a rather grainy and fuzzy reproduction, but then the state of the art. In any case, something had gone wrong and we now had to do the commercial over again.

Chester was called back just as he was about to leave for home, and it was evident that his flask was empty and he was feeling little pain. However, his embarrassment and panic were clearly visible.

We began the commercial and try as he may, Chester's words didn't come out right. Then when they did, he had them in the wrong place. He was now chagrined beyond belief, and, almost in tears, he said, "Alan, I assure you I have never taken a show before a drink." With that, we all broke up, including Chester. I wonder, are these gorgeous people still around?

Even back then, I tried to work with animals as much as possible. They were always good for laughs and it gave a variety to the show. We had written an African sketch using the famous old actor Wally Ford. In this sketch I played his houseboy, assisted by a trained chimpanzee. At the beginning of the scene, I am sitting with the chimp, explaining his household duties.

During the dress rehearsal, the chimp entered on cue and sat beside me on the bench. I began explaining things to him and he suddenly put his arm over my shoulder and stared at me. I figured all was going well so I continued my instructions. The animal began touching my face with its other hand and I heard muffled, then loud guffaws from the orchestra pit. I still didn't know what was going on, but was aware that the chimp's actions were now becoming more and more amorous. It was then I looked down and saw that the chimp really had the hots for me and was showing it in more ways than one. We cut the rehearsal short, and the trainer removed the chimp for a cold shower, or whatever they do to horny primates.

About an hour later, the trainer reported that all was well, so we tried the rehearsal once more. This time the chimp entered, took a look at me and with a joyous "whoo" he jumped on the bench and picked up where he left off. The band went into hysterics, but we were desperate. We had a lovesick monkey and it was too late to replace him.

Finally, our prop man came to the rescue. "I'll take care of things," he said.

As there was only a few minutes left before airtime, we put our trust in him and went off to make-up. The show began and, when it came time for the chimp's entrance, I subtly crossed my fingers. This got a snicker from the musicians who were watching in anticipation. The chimp entered, slowly and unhappily. He was evidently wearing some sort of diaper, bound tightly with electrician's tape, and painted to match his hair.

The band couldn't contain themselves and roared. The audience, sensing something funny, joined in. The monkey stared miserably. He got on the bench as I began my monologue. His expressions ranged from sadness to frustration and to misery, thwarted desire and frustrated love, perfectly fitting reactions to my speech.

Later, I was asked how on earth they got a chimpanzee to express such consummate emotions.

"Oh, you've just got to know how to handle them," I answered.

"Yeah, you sure have a way with animals. They really love you, right?"

"Oh yes!"

Oh, those Golden Days!

GEORGE BURNS

In the late forties, I lived at the Hollywood Plaza Hotel, across the street from the Brown Derby and two blocks north of NBC. George Burns had his offices on one of the top floors of the hotel where the writers met and put together the *Burns and Allen* radio show. This is where I learned what a great editor of comedy George was, and what an uncanny talent he had for the proper presentation of a gag.

His radio show was never number one. But, as he said, "If you're number one and fall to number two, the critics say you're slipping. But if you're fifth or sixth they don't notice." Consequently, the *Burns and Allen Show* was always in the top ten.

He also had a canny finger on the public's pulse. In the days of radio, each comic had a catch phrase which invariably drew laughs from the audience. One day, one of the writers said to George, "Let's not use that line again this week. We're all getting tired of it."

George took a drag on his cigar. "What we're getting tired of, the public is just catching on. We'll keep doing it."

The result was: "Say 'goodnight,' Gracie," said George. "Goodnight, Gracie," said Gracie.

And we're still not tired of it! Burns and Allen started in television in 1951. I remember well because I shared the same stage with them as well as the same director and crew. The director, Ralph Levy, was very concerned when George insisted on smoking his cigar during the introduction of the show and throughout the narration. It wasn't because of the smoking, but when George took the cigar out of his mouth, as he always did to punctuate a line, the chewed end of the stogie was anything but appetizing, especially in a close-up.

Finally, Ralph approached the matter diplomatically, but with great trepidation, knowing that George did not hesitate to voice his opinion and displeasure quite cogently.

"Mr. Burns," he said hesitatingly, "I have a slight problem in photographing you."

Being new to TV, George was instantly concerned. "Yeah? What's the problem?"

"Well, you are such a fastidious dresser." (Which is true. I never saw George without perfectly creased trousers, matching socks, shined shoes, manicured fingernails. He was a fashion plate.)

"So what?" said George. "That's a problem?"

"No," Ralph continued. "It's just that with your immaculate appearance it looks a little incongruous when we take a close up of the chewed, wet end of the cigar."

Much to Ralph's relief, George always listened to reason. On the next show, his cigar sported the plastic tip which was evident for the next thirty-five years of his performances.

George Burns trying out the new plastic cigar tips.

"This green plot shall be our stage"
(Shakespeare)

I was playing dinner theatre in Texas. My co-star, Jim . . . , may not have been a great actor, but his love of the theatre and its history was to him more important than a good performance.

State show in Florida, 1949.

Jim suddenly asked me one day, "Did you know that a hundred years ago, actors had to have special passes to ride in the stagecoach with other people?"

"So, where's the progress?" I said. "We still can't join the Los Angeles Athletic Club."

"I can't get into the Diner's Club," Jim said. "Or the American Express."

We had just arrived at an apartment the theater had rented for us to live in during the run of our play in Texas. It was clean enough and fairly well furnished, but a large placard stating "Rules of Order" in three-inch letters stood stark and glaring on the kitchen table. Scrawled across the entire page in black crayon was the admonition: "NO PETS!"

Just then, we were surprised as the manager poked her head in the room. (What surprised us was that she poked it in on a stick.) Her name was Ozella Huntoon, and something about her told us she didn't like actors. It was her mouth. It opened up and told us. "I don't like actors," it said. Then it added, "I don't like animals. You are not allowed any animals."

"You excite me when you make demands like that, ma'me," Jim said passionately. "Was your husband in the Navy?"

"I don't have one," she answered.

"Of course you do," Jim said. "Everybody has a Navy. That's where our taxes go."

"I'm talking about a husband," she snapped. "I don't have one; never have, never will."

"Is that so," I said. "I thought you just weren't allowed animals."

Ozella had had enough of this repartee and she started out. "No wild parties, no drugs and no animals!" she thundered and left. Now, Jim is a good friend, but a heck of an enemy, and Ozella had just cultivated him in the latter capacity.

"I'll fix her," he said. "Oh, I don't know how yet, but it'll come to me."

It came to him that night as we were driving back to the apartment after the show.

Strand Theatre, 1949. It was work and I was grateful to get it.

"What's that dog doing over there?" he asked suddenly.

I looked and spotted a large spaniel squatting on the sidewalk in an obvious posture. "It's either a back problem or he's having a bowel movement," I said.

Jim pulled the car over and began rummaging through the glove compartment. "That's it," he said. "That's it! Now if I can just find — ha!"

He took a plastic bag from the compartment, got out of the car and headed for the spot the dog had just left. Twenty minutes later, the tiny lawn between our apartment and the manager's office was sporting its first special delivery.

The next day we bought a couple of "pooper-scoopers" from a pet shop. This made our collecting a little more sanitary and secretive. Now, of course, we weren't satisfied with just one touch, but could decorate the lawn with more careless abandon.

At first, Ozella's curiosity was subtle. She would peer casually into our window, or give our small patio an offhand scrutiny. By the fourth day, however, when the lawn looked like it had been visited by an itinerant wolf-pack, Ozella was fuming.

"All right," she boomed through our door. "Who has the dog? I know it's here."

Jim opened the door and smiled a welcome you could ice a cake with. "A dog, Miss Huntoon? But that's against the rules."

He opened the door a little further and Ozella's eyes widened. "A-ha, what's that?" she roared.

A large chewed bone lay by the sofa just where we'd placed it. I picked it up and began gnawing. "We're just having a snack before turning in."

Jim took a large messy-looking T-bone from behind his back and began nibbling delicately. Ozella left, making strange guttural noises.

Now our imaginations had no barriers. Next day we stopped at a small farm, and contributions of horse, cow, rabbit and an entire chicken coop were included in our regular delivery. In the afternoon, the lawn had been a pristine pool of green without speck or blemish. Next morning it looked like Noah had made a pit stop. Here we should have ceased all activity and let the event pass into Texas theatrical history. But Jim, with true artistic obsession, had to add that one last finishing touch which indicates either a genius or a klutz. Three guesses.

We bought a box of heavy-duty garbage bags and took off for the children's zoo. Happily mumbling "A rose is a rose is a rose," Jim shoveled ecstatically while I held the bag, begging him to shut up and watch his aim. It took three hours of stealthy stealing, bagging and carrying, but finally the back of the VW was piled from floor to ceiling with our steaming load. The donations represented every animal in the zoo from aardvark to zebra; each separated, tabulated and insulated. Even driving with the windows open, it still seemed as though we were being closely followed by Grizzly Adams. I couldn't believe my nose.

Nearing our building, Jim slowed the car. "Oh no," he gasped. "Take a look."

Parked in our driveway was a security car. A uniformed guard was hammering a sign into the lawn which announced in large letters that the grounds were now guarded by a 24-hour patrol. Ozella had struck back.

"Now what do we do with this load?" Jim asked.

A large dog, sniffing keenly, came up to my side of the car. I noticed several more dogs approaching from the rear. They were panting and drooling and must have been following us for blocks.

"First, we better get out of here," I said. "And roll up the windows. We're sending nasal messages to every dog in Texas and most of Arkansas."

We put up the windows and drove off. Now the combination of 90-degree weather, plus our combustible contraband, created a definite ground-fog inside the car. The windows began clouding up.

"Where are we gonna go?" Jim asked. "Back to the zoo? We can't return this stuff."

"We can throw ourselves on their mercy," I said. "Besides, what are they going to charge us with — stealing? The best they can get us on is second-degree littering. And hurry up. The dogs are gaining!"

Jim looked in the rear-view mirror. "We've got more than that after us. There's a police car and he's flashing his lights. We've gotta stop."

"Well, for God's sake, don't open the window. Wave at him through the glass."

The officer walked up and stood by the door. "Roll your window down," he yelled. "I think your radiator has boiled over."

"Nothing's wrong, officer," Jim called back to him, peering through the mist. "The car's just getting broken in."

The cop stared. "It's a 1953," he said.

Then the policeman opened the door. This was an act he would have given his salary to buy back. The steamy vapor enveloped him like a malodorous mantle, instantly tarnishing his badge and peeling the varnish off his visor. It also took his voice away for a few moments. Then it returned, quiet and ominous.

"I'm sure there's an explanation for this," he said.

"Okay," said Jim. "Let's hear it."

That did it. Within half an hour, we were sitting in a cell in the solitary wing, having been moved there at the request of the other prisoners.

Our clothing was examined, fumigated, and we were deloused. Our car was now in the hands of the bomb-disposal unit. For a while, the narcotics' division thought we were growing something, homicide thought we were trying to kill something, and everyone within three blocks thought we had killed something. It was getting close to showtime and we were desperate.

"I told you what we did," Jim said. "We robbed the zoo."

"We checked the zoo," said the police sergeant. "They say there's nothing missing."

"Well, it's not the kind of thing they keep tabs on," Jim explained. His voice was several decibels higher and it was quite noticeable.

"Your voice is several decibels higher," said the sergeant. "I noticed it."

"Well, you don't believe our story," I said.

"Your story is okay," replied the sergeant. "But your evidence has a certain air of incredibility."

I admired his cool rationality, and I told him so. "I admire your cool rational —," I began.

"Oh, shut up," he said. "I'm not talking to you. Besides, you have a definite overbite."

Sensing a slight antipathy, I walked over to the water cooler and began cooling my water. I know when an impasse has been reached. You take Highway 134 to the Pasadena Freeway, then cut off on Colorado Boulevard. You can't miss it. The sergeant had been thumbing through the criminal code for a while and now he suddenly lit his feet and jumped to a cigarette.

"There's no case here," he announced. "Nobody filed a complaint of stolen — er — articles. Whatever you picked up had been duly discarded. The worse we could get you on is flotsam and jetsam, and that charge only holds water if you're in it."

We left. It took a while to get rid of the evidence from the car, and a longer time to rid the car of the evidence of the evidence. But it was all worth it. We had struck a blow for the actor's equity. The message was simple for all who can read and understand:

TO THE POLICE: If an actor is behind the wheel it could be a hot car in more ways than one.

TO APARTMENT MANAGERS: Whatever you hand out to an actor will come back to you in spades — or shovels.

TO THE ACTOR: Never ignore what someone has
                                 discarded. It may be your best
                                 weapon.

———◆———

One December in 1976 I was appearing in a play at the
Pheasant Run dinner theater just west of Chicago. It was a
small stage and in our production, the set took up the entire
space, right up to the back wall. Actors making an entrance
stage-right were okay, but any entrance from stage-left meant
that the actor had to go out the fire door, into the parking lot,
cross behind the theater and enter from an outside door
directly on the stage.

Everything was working out just fine until the Chicago area
was hit by one of the worst storms in history. Snow piled up
quickly and by the time our curtain went up, there was at least
three feet around the theater, drifting to six feet against the
wall. I was on stage alone, talking on the telephone and,
during the conversation, I said, "Well, Fred, I'll have to hang
up now. I hear Charlie coming downstairs. He must have slept
late." This was the cue for the actor to enter. I turned toward
the archway where "Charlie" was going to appear. No one was
there, but I could hear muffled sounds coming from outside
the fire door. In a frantic reflex, I quickly picked up the
phone.

"Oh, good, Fred, you're still on the line." I adlibbed desperately.
I'm sure the audience marveled at the peculiarly efficient phone
service.

"That wasn't Charlie," I continued. "It was, er, well, it certainly
wasn't Charlie. He generally stays in bed till noon. In fact
sometimes he sleeps until one or two."

Still, the muffled thumps, and no entrance, so I continued
my account of Charlie's sleeping habits, especially during these
hot summer months! Suddenly, the door burst open and Charlie
made an exploding, stormy entrance. The spectacle brought

the house down. Charlie stood there in his dripping pajamas. He was covered with snow, his slippers were soaking and he had a wreath of snow covering his head. The view couldn't be ignored.

"What happened to you?" I asked, using the thespians' prerogative to dump the problem onto a fellow actor.

He was quick, or perhaps he'd been working on an ad-lib while fighting through the snowdrifts. "We've gotta fix that air conditioner," he said. "It's gone crazy up there!"

The audience didn't buy it but he received an ovation.

JOHN CHARLES THOMAS

Whenever President Roosevelt was being honored, which happened frequently, the orchestra would greet him with "Home on the Range." This was acknowledged to be his favorite song. The man who sang it, in fact, had a monopoly on the number, the famous concert singer John Charles Thomas.

Thomas had a robust, booming bass baritone that sounded like the *QE2* docking. In later years, President Roosevelt finally admitted that he couldn't stand the song, but it was too late. Thomas knew all the words and wasn't about to stop singing it.

Years later, I was appearing at a benefit and took along my bagpipes. Thomas was also on the show and, making conversation, I told him I could play "Home on the Range" on the pipes.

"Great idea," he said. "You can accompany me!"

I tried to tell him that the bagpipes were too loud for the human voice; even his. At that he roared.

"I've never been drowned out yet," he laughed. "If that ever happens, I'll go into another business!"

So we did it. The orchestra played the introduction, Thomas began and he got out the words "Oh give me a home —," then the bagpipes struck in. His eyes widened, his chin dropped and he just stared. He turned and walked off the stage. I thought, "Dear God, I've offended that great man."

But he was greater than I thought. He returned to the stage

carrying a broom and began humbly sweeping the stage, indicating he'd gone into another business!

◆

I had my first and only contact with "the mob" in November of 1948 while playing a Detroit nightclub. Mobsters are great fans of show people for a multitude of reasons. Why Abe Bernstein decided to befriend me, I have no idea, except I was the only comic playing in town at the time.

Appearing at the Pantages Theatre with Gloria De Haven, 1951.

Abe was the head of "The Purple Gang." This colorful group was famous for its method of dispatching anyone who crossed them or attracted their wrath. No guns, knives or garrotes for them. These extreme measures were too traceable. They simply took their victims up to the roof of the highest and handiest building and encouraged the poor soul to jump.

I met a Detroit disc jockey who had sold papers outside the Book Cadillac Hotel as a young boy and he reported that on several occasions, he heard a scream from above, and then a splat. If he heard coins rolling around, he headed for the drop; if not, he said he'd rather not look.

When I first met Abe, he invited me to have tea with him at the Book Cadillac Hotel. "It's a nice place," he said. "And they have a fashion show."

I figured "fashion show" was an aphorism for some swinging frolic that gangsters enjoyed. I was surprised to find that it was tea and a fashion show with beautiful young ladies, some of whom Abe seemed to know fairly well. While there, he received an urgent phone message and he asked if I'd mind going with him to attend a meeting for a few minutes before he dropped me off. I assured him that I was in no hurry so he took me along.

Seated in a basement room of a dingy building were a dozen or so of the roughest characters I've ever seen. There wasn't an unbroken nose in the place. Abe looked like an alien with his hand-tailored suit, razor-sharp creased trousers, lapel flower and Homburg. A serious labor strike had been taking place for weeks in most of the local plants, and this deadlock was being discussed. I was introduced to a brother or brother-in-law of our then-President Truman, who was either an arbiter or negotiator. Whichever he was, he was getting nowhere, and a huge man with hands like the jaws of life was gesturing wildly and complaining to Abe that "some kinda action had to be took." His hands and gestures left no doubt as to what sort of action he was espousing.

After listening to the threats and mumbles of approval from the gathered goons, Abe waited until they fell silent, then he turned to Jaws and quietly responded, "Settle the strike."

There was a negative murmur from the goons, and the giant said, "But Abe, the negotiations are —"

It was then I saw why Abe was the boss. This little man seemed to zoom to six-foot-ten and loom over the group.

"Settle it," he hissed.

They voted 12 to 0 to settle.

A few days later, the nightclub and movie comedian Ben Blue came to Detroit. He was also an acquaintance of Abe's and he came to him for assistance. While working in town some months previously, he had bought a new car and from the beginning it was nothing but trouble. Constant visits to the dealership brought no satisfaction and everyone agreed it was a lemon and nothing could be done.

"Sure it can," said Abe, and he called one of his associates over. "Drive Ben and Alan over to the dealership and make sure they're taken care of."

The man, whose face looked like he had just run into a door, nodded and led us to his car. He parked next to a vacant lot near the dealership, which was an impressive building with a magnificent curved-glass showroom window. Puzzled, Ben and I watched as our friend searched through the vacant lot. Then he gave a satisfied grunt and picked up a large boulder.

"Let's go," he said, and we walked toward the leadership.

About fifteen feet from the window he stopped and drew back his arm. Panicked, Ben grabbed him. "What are you gonna do?" he asked.

"I'm gonna trow dis rock tru that window," he answered, as if explaining to a child. "First they gotta know ya mean business."

Ben took the rock from him and we entered the showroom. He asked for the manager and, as Ben was highly recognizable in those days, the manager appeared immediately.

"Yes, Mr. Blue," he said sympathetically. "We still having difficulty with the car?"

"Yeah," Ben replied. "Mr. Abe Bernstein sent his attorney with me to negotiate. I just stopped him from throwing this rock through your front window."

The manager paled, stared, then hurried to his office. That afternoon, Ben had a new top-of-the-line car to drive back to California.

Before I left Detroit, Abe gave me a handwritten list of people in every major city to whom I could turn if I ever needed help. In my home state of California was a man named Sammis, and shortly after, I read a magazine article in which Governor Earl Warren stated, "Sammis wields more power in the State that I do."

I never used the list because you never know when the helping hand may have a rock in it!

———◆———

Through ASCAP, a composer's work is protected from theft. Registering a story or play protects the writer from having his work plagiarized. There is no such protection for a comedian's material or the variety performer's act. Many years ago, I bought a three-minute piece of sure-fire material from Jackie Barnett, a composer and creator of variety acts. Through the years, I witnessed and heard of some performers doing this piece of my material with great success. In desperation, I went to a dear friend, Joe Besser, for his advice. Joe had been in Vaudeville all his life, his act being a hilarious rookie soldier routine, later adapted for Abbott and Costello's first starring motion picture. Joe ended his career as one of the famous Three Stooges.

"How can I copyright my material, Joe?" I asked. "People are doing my 'The Horse' recitation and now, if I perform it, the audience will think I stole it."

"You can't legally register an act," he said. "But there is a way of protecting it."

I later heard how Joe did it. When he was playing the New York Paramount Theater, he learned that a new comic opened at the Capitol, three blocks north, and was doing much of Joe's routine. Joe paid a visit to the Capitol, stood backstage and quietly watched the comic performing his act word for word and action for action. The act finished and, to great applause, the comic ran off stage into the wings. Joe stepped out and decked him in mid-flight. The man ended up back on stage, flat on his behind.

"There," Joe called to him. "I just exercised my copyright!"

———◦◆◦———

In the twenties (I wasn't there, but it is a well-told story in my English hometown) there were many "pub performers" — men who had learned one trick or another that they practiced for the only purpose of having free drinks bought for them. Some of the amateur artists were quite skilled and not particularly modest about it. One of them, "Wizard Willie" as he loved to be called, perfected several magic tricks that had kept him in village acclaim and free booze for many years.

One day the newspaper announced that the great American magician Houdini would be appearing at the Newcastle Empire the following week. Willie was incensed. Another magician was going to invade his turf? "I can do anything he can," said Willie.

He had read about Houdini and his various escape sensations and had figured them out carefully, or so he thought. The pub habitués felt that this might be an opportunity for a little wager war and took him up on his boasts. Some believed Willie, had confidence in him, and others did not. This made for enthusiastic betting.

Willie decided that he would perform one of Houdini's own dramatic escape demonstrations and do it the day before the Newcastle appearance, thereby showing the native populace that the great Houdini had nothing on the local Willie.

"I'll need help," he said to his pub associates. "I want you to find lads who have stage experience to be my assistants."

This was done, and the day before Houdini's opening, Willie appeared at a rival theater which was crowded with his supporters, doubters, and the non-committed — in fact, almost the whole population of Newcastle.

Willie appeared majestically on stage to the cheers of his fans. His assistants bound him, locked him in a trunk, and hoisted him high in the air above the stage. A drum roll sounded and the escape began. The trunk rocked and swayed as the drum roll swelled and ebbed and the audience "ooohed" and waited. They waited, and the trunk rocked while the drum rolled. Soon it was evident that the drummer was tiring as the roll ebbed more than it swelled. Finally it stopped altogether and the audience waited in silence. This evidently became a little oppressive and many began to leave and head for their favorite "local," figuring that Willie would be along as soon as he had made his great escape.

It never happened.

The next morning, what was left of his supporters lowered the trunk and released a tired, beaten Wizard Willie. It was later found the reason for his dismal failure. The assistants who had been hired were two of Houdini's aides, who had arrived the day before to prepare for the show.

From then on Willie had to buy his own drinks.

Until the late 1950s, most Hollywood studios had a stock contract-player system. Young men and women were put on a small salary, then trained in acting, riding, fencing, dancing etc. If they were lucky, they got a small part in one of the studio's productions and they were on their way — up or out. The girls were named "starlets," and this shining beacon to fame and fortune attracted young maiden butterflies who came from every corner of America. About one in a thousand managed to sign a contract, generally a six-month arrangement, and when their option was not picked up, they joined the flocks of fluttering, failing destitute butterflies. It was hard to return to their homes and admit failure, so generally the girls headed for temporary jobs as waitresses, or receptionists, any part-time job that would enable them to press on with their "careers." A few less selective but more ambitious girls chose to enter the oldest profession and were soon making more money than most stars with contracts.

My friend, I'll call him Henry because he doesn't need the publicity, was an assistant producer at that time. He had been married but was now enjoying the bachelors' life, alone but not lonely, yet still looking. He had dated the starlets and seen the frustrated ambition in their eyes, so now he was quietly waiting for someone more settled.

Then, while pushing a shopping cart through the vegetable department, he saw her over the broccoli. She was stunning, classic, well dressed but not flashy with just enough make-up to enhance her natural beauty. She saw him staring at her and smiled briefly, then moved on. Henry was momentarily frozen. When he came to, she was gone, so he grabbed his cart and sped down the aisles in search of his vision. Rounding a corner, his cart almost knocked over. "Oh Gosh, sorry," he gasped. "I was hoping to bump into you again, but not this way!"

She laughed, which broke the ice nicely, and that started the conversation. Before Henry left the store, he had her address, with the promise that maybe they could enjoy a drink later. That evening, he arrived promptly at her apartment, to find her waiting outside the building. They had a delightful hour or two together, and she promised to go out with him the next night for dinner. Then again the following night and as always she met him outside.

The friendship grew into romance. The sex was great and many times she proved herself a great cook by preparing dinner, but always at his apartment. He still had never been in hers. Finally one evening she called and said she wanted to see him and would he come to her place. Henry lost not a moment. Her apartment was tastefully decorated, the dinner was great and in no time they were in the bedroom experiencing the after-dinner-delights in her king-sized bed.

Just as Henry was about to ask for seconds, there was a tremendous crash as the front door was broken in and mens' voices were heard. The girl jumped out of bed. "My God," she cried. "It's the vice squad!"

"The what?" Henry yelled, grabbing for his pants. He was a little too late as several policemen barged into the bedroom.

"Hold it right there, Shorty," said a cop. The inference was not lost on Henry's ego.

The policeman turned to the girl. "You're under arrest, lady, both you and your John."

On the way to the police station, Henry learned the whole story. His date was one of the best-known and most successful prostitutes in West Hollywood, and the police department had been instructed to crack down on not only the hookers but the customers. He would join her in jail until the trial.

"I'm innocent," Henry screamed. "I didn't know what she was." Then he added triumphantly, "No money changed hands."

"You could be on the Diner's Club and signed for it," the cop replied. "Now shut up."

As Henry was being taken to a jail cell, he demanded to be able to call his lawyer. Within an hour, the lawyer arrived and posted bail.

"What about the girl?" Henry asked his lawyer.

"You want to go bail for her too?"

Now Henry is a good egg and, hooker or not, he had enjoyed her company and couldn't bear to think of her being locked up.

"Okay, I'll take care of it," his lawyer said. "It may take a little time, but I'll get you both out. Just wait here."

"Do I have a choice?" Henry said, sitting in a jail cell for the first time in his life.

By the time the lawyer returned, Henry was steaming. Even his release failed to cool him down. "Do you know what I'm gonna do?" he asked his lawyer. "I'm gonna sue the police department for false arrest, humiliation and . . ."

The lawyer shook his head. "You can't," he said. "The police now realize you weren't a John but in order to get you out, I struck a deal. They release you both and you don't sue."

About this time the girl appeared. She rushed up and kissed Henry, "Oh thank you, Henry. You did a wonderful thing."

"Naw, it was nothing," Henry replied modestly.

"Oh, but it was," she persisted. "You see, I've never been in jail in my life. And if my husband ever found out . . . !"

Henry has never remarried. Nor does he do his own shopping anymore. He phones and has everything delivered.

Why are they called "practical jokes"? I don't think they're very practical, at least not in the common sense, and to those on the receiving end, they're certainly no joke. I tried one once and it backfired so badly that I never tried again.

It all began back in the forties. I had just performed a benefit performance in the then-popular "Police Show." Each year the L.A.P.D. put on a huge show in the Shrine Auditorium. It ran for a week and the proceeds went to support widows and orphans, which the police department sponsored. Stars made guest appearances and, in gratitude, they were presented with an authentic police badge. At least it looked authentic until you looked closely and saw that it said, "Gratefully presented to . . .," with the date of the show. The badge didn't have any practical application but made an attractive conversation ornament. Until I found a use for it.

Sometime later I was writing my television show in concert with two other men. One of them was a great writer but, at times, unreliable, especially if he'd had a belt or two, or had a sudden desire for female company. He was particularly fond of a comfort house, run by three ex-starlets who found this new-old occupation much more rewarding than working for a hundred dollars a week at the studio, and putting out for some of the executives for a kiss and a promise.

One day we were just about to finish a script, and "George" was missing. (For confidentiality I have given him this pseudonym. His real name is Charlie.) In the middle of the afternoon, he phoned the office and after a quick apology, said that a friend and he had paid a visit to the "house" and the friend had left, leaving George without a car or a drive to the office. Would I pick him up?

Of course I agreed and he gave me the address. It was one of the delightful little houses, nestled cozily in the Hollywood Hills, just east of Laurel Canyon. As I drove there, my annoyance turned to amusement at my friend's predicament, then it all slowly turned to a diabolical idea. "He should be taught a lesson," I thought. "And I think I have with me the very thing."

I arrived at the house and rang the doorbell. I could smell the perfume as one of the girls was approaching. The door opened and there stood a blonde beauty. "Come in," she said seductively. "I know you're Alan and my name is '………….'" I recognized the name and the face from pin-up pictures released by the studio. Her figure rang a bell too.

As she shut the door, Charlie entered sheepishly. "I'm all set, Alan," he said.

"Well, I'm not," I snapped. "I have a little business to attend to."

With that, I unzipped my fly. Charlie gasped. The girls smiled approvingly, business was picking up. I reached in and pulled out my shirttail. Attached and hanging from it was my police badge, shining in all its splendor. "This is a raid," I said. "What can I tell you?"

I expected a shocked reaction, then a laugh all around, but being young, a little naive, and not having been in a place of this kind, I reckoned wrong. The girl let out a scream and ran out of the room. Her screams brought the other girls running, along with their clients in various states of dress or undress. When they entered the living room, they all froze in their tracks and stared as I stood there speechless, my shirt and badge dangling provocatively.

"It's a raid, a raid!" the girl kept yelling hysterically.

Only Charlie had his wits about him, having undoubtedly been in this position before. "Come on, Eliot Ness," he said. "Let's go."

We drove a while in silence and then I found myself apologizing to him. "Forget it, boss," he said magnanimously. "Now put your badge back in and zip up your fly.

≕ Chapter Nine ≕
The Time Machine

Thanks to television, VHS and the DVD, the 1960 release of *The Time Machine* has become a popular classic. Faithful fans of the original picture E-mail me with requests to talk about the making of the movie and tell the story of the original and the

Filby was my favorite character because he was so much like my dad.

This is the most touching scene in the film and seems to be everyone's favorite.

recent remake. The original *Time Machine* was one of the most unheralded, underestimated, unfunded pictures Hollywood ever ignored. The following is the story. MGM evidently had a pittance of profits frozen in Britain so they let George Pal use it to make a picture. The production was *tom thumb*, one of the most unheralded, underestimated unpublicized, um — well, you get the picture. I was living in England at the time and, as George wanted an American actor in the film, and as I was available and would work for scale, he hired me. George and I got along beautifully, and why not? He was one of the nicest, unheralded, under — same thing. He said, "Alan, I'll make it up to you on my next picture. I'm going to make H.G. Wells' *Time Machine* and want you in it."

Evidently the studio's British money was used up, so George was given the go-ahead to shoot it in Hollywood.

When he phoned me he said, "My budget is smaller than *tom thumb's* so I can't pay you as much as I did before." I didn't care. It was work. I needed it. And he promised I could do anything I wanted with the character. I patterned him after my father, a gentle, loyal Scotsman, who would be the perfect confidante to the "Time Traveler." I had never seen a single frame when they were filming, so when it was released, I couldn't wait to finally see it. After much searching, I found it playing in a small theater in a secluded section of the San Fernando Valley.

As I said, its opening had all the impact of a caterpillar backing into a thick rug.

Now, let's time travel forward to the 2002 version of the same picture. Evidently, the producers of the remake, became aware of the fact that out there somewhere, was a host of fans of the original production. In no way did they intend or want to alienate that large audience. They contacted me and asked if I could help in their promotion and be a bridge between *Time Machine* I and II.

Photo: Carol Summers

2003. What are we smiling about? Rod Taylor and I haven't sold a picture!

There was no payment involved, but I felt that it was the right thing to do. I feel it's what George Pal would have done, loving his "baby" as he did. They introduced me to the great cast that was assembled. Then they showed me the fabulous sets and the unbelievable machine they had constructed. I was amazed and thought George Pal would have loved to have a budget like this!

To continue this "bridge" between the two productions, the producers asked if I would make an appearance in their picture. A cameo wasn't possible as the script was finished. So, I agreed to do a "Hitchcock" — a tiny walk-on appearance.

I attended the picture's preview and the result was obvious to all. George Pal's modest sets and production emulated perfectly the simplicity of H.G. Wells' uncomplicated story. The turn of the century was a quiet, somewhat gentle time. Even the villainous appearance of the Morlocks, was a short and rather subdued event. Compared with *TM* I, the ambitious production of *TM* II, was a stark, shocking contrast. It was as if a magnifying glass was held against Pal's underplayed scenes and enlarged 100 times. It was a truly astounding example of present day's technological advancement into the spectacular. In the conception of the remake, they left out the heart.

Coming out of the theater, one could feel the disappointment. An excellent cast, talented director, and well-meaning producers, were now aware of the fact that Thoreau's advice, "Simplify, simplify," is a wise path to follow.

SCROOGE MCDUCK

In countless clubs throughout the United States, groups have been formed, dedicated to old radio.

I have been invited to some of these conventions and must say that they are the most enthusiastic fans I've ever seen. They elect directors, publish newsletters and glossy periodicals, all dedicated to radio nostalgia.

From archives, they obtain old radio scripts, and at their conventions, they produce first class re-broadcasts of top radio classics. They sometimes even involve the original stars.

Amazingly, this is not just the result of old-timers nostalgia, because I have noticed that most of the enthusiasts were not even born when radio was at its peak. These people realize radio's history and what an impact it had on the public.

Radio took performers from the stage and brought them into our living rooms. People who either couldn't afford the price of a theatre ticket or lived miles away from a city, could suddenly enjoy performers they had only read about. As far as actors were concerned, the experience gained from performing in radio

Scrooge McDuck © 2006 and TM Disney Enterprises, Inc.

provided a versatility that can never be taught. Using the voice to create a character, provides an actor with a treasure-trove of vocal abilities.

During a lull in my employment, an executive from the Walt Disney recording division called me.

"You wrote for radio, didn't you?" he asked.

"Yes, that's how I started in this business," I said.

He then told me that the Studio had produced an album of Christmas carols sung by various Disney characters. Evidently the idea was great, but the result was not. In fact, it was not up to Disney standards, so they cancelled its release. However, now they were stuck with thousands of expensive album covers . . . a loss which they were loathe to absorb.

"We've decided to produce a recording of Charles Dickens' *A Christmas Carol* he said. Can you write and produce it?"

When a performer is out of work, he says "yes" to everything.

And so I was stuck with the project. I say "stuck" because the album cover had drawings of the various Disney characters so they must all be included in the story. Disney was a stickler for honesty. So, as it turned out, Mickey, Minnie, Goofy, Donald, Huey, Dewey, and Louie, all had to fit in.

I hired a small studio in Santa Monica and we were off. Scrooge was easy to cast. My real name is Angus and I came from that bonny land. I also played Mickey and I later received a letter from the head of the Studio saying I was the first to do the voice of Mickey since Walt Disney had done it. Doing Mickey was no great feat. I just imitated Walt. The rest of the cast was made up of all Disney voices and were naturally perfect. The album sold out, as did the subsequent tapes.

Disney decided to make a spin-off called *DuckTales*, starring Scrooge McDuck. Meanwhile, I was playing dinner theatre. One evening while putting on my makeup, I overheard my acting partner, Dennis James, mumbling aloud the lines he was attempting to conquer.

"Alan," he said finally. "You're Scottish, aren't you?"

"Yes". He passed a script over to me. "I'm auditioning for this

Scrooge McDuck © 2006 and TM Disney Enterprises, Inc.

tomorrow, and I don't do a Scots accent. Can you help me?"

I looked at the script. It was exactly the one I had written for *Christmas Carol*. The next day, after coaching Dennis, I phoned the Disney casting department.

"I'm Alan Young," I said. "And if you will allow me, I'd like to read for the part of Scrooge McDuck".

The man was apologetic. "Of course," he said. "We didn't think you'd want to do this, so we didn't ask."

I auditioned and got it. The *DuckTales* production was a return to the original classic Disney animation style. Each cell was beautifully painted. It wasn't a cartoon. It was a new and artistic form of a children's animated program. And as yet, it has not been duplicated.

DuckTales has been a gold-mine for Disney; and though Mickey may get all the credit, Scrooge doesn't mind. He is quacking all the way to the bank!

EPILOGUE
"IT WAS EASIER THEN"

A young girl was complaining to me about the difficulties of getting into show business.

"It's always been a challenge," I agreed.

"Oh, but not like it is now," she said. "Now there's so much competition. It was easier back then."

Easier then? I thought of my experience which, I am sure, is duplicated by many of my contemporaries. I lived in a small Canadian town. There was no live theatre, no acting schools, nightclubs, etc. Saying that your ambition was to become an actor in my town was like a kid from Brooklyn saying he wanted to become a shepherd.

I always had great faith and trust. I believed that God created man and designed a purpose for him. He wouldn't created ten men and only nine purposes. God doesn't play "musical chairs" with His creation.

One evening I was alone in my room performing one of my routines to nobody in particular. I imitated people I had heard on the radio, jokes and all. I wasn't aware of the fact that a neighbor dropped in to visit my mother. She heard my performance and said to Mother: "This kid has to have an audience."

Two days later the neighbor and I were on a fifty-mile drive to the big city. Radio station CJOR in Vancouver had a Saturday variety show called *The Bathtub Review*, which was open to any performer wanting to display his talents. They liked what they heard and I was booked on the show every week. No pay, of course, but later they hired me as an office-boy. Then I worked my way into being "assistant to the program director." This high title simply meant that I answered the phones, typed out scripts, played bit parts and got coffee.

In the late evening CJOR put various dance bands on the air to fill in time. The station had only one standing mike to spare, so it was my job to take it to the dance hall, plug it in, then later unplug it and transport it to the next dance hall. Unfortunately, I had no car and didn't know how to drive anyway, so the streetcar was my alternative. Boarding a street car with a cumbersome standing mike is a challenge at best, but in a crowd it's almost impossible. The crowd pushed ahead of me and I just managed to get the top of the mike in when the doors closed. I was left outside holding the base of the mike with the main part stuck in the door. The streetcar started up and I had to run alongside with a death-grip on my precious cargo. As the dance hall was on the edge of town, the streetcar's next stop was a good quarter of a mile away during which time it started to rain — and rain in Vancouver means RAIN! I got to the dance hall soaked to the skin carrying a soggy mike. When they plugged it in, it short-circuited and blew all the lights in the hall. I was later relieved of this responsibility.

My next assignment almost ended my budding radio career. I didn't realize that the title "office boy" meant I was fair game for everybody to use as an assistant.

The sports announcer needed help at the wrestling matches. I had never seen wrestling and was very excited at the prospect. Sitting ringside was a traumatic experience and I couldn't believe what I saw. The announcer hadn't told me that the bout was a well-rehearsed athletic exhibition, so the head-butts, body slams, kicks and punches had me gasping.

One of the wrestlers held a few phoney teeth in the side of his mouth. After receiving a fake, but impressive punch in the jaw, he spat out the fake teeth, red dye and all. I gasped!

The other man had a tiny nail secreted in his trunks and, in the midst of the violent writhing, he unintentionally scratched his own forehead. With a loud wail he stood up with blood streaming down his face. I retched. His opponent then picked him up, spun him around and threw him out of the ring. He landed on the apron directly above me, moaning and bleeding.

The announcer was excitedly describing the action at the top of his voice. The crowd was screaming with animalistic delight. The blood sprayed onto my shirt, and that was all I could take. I threw up all over the prone "Saskatoon Strangler."

Yep. It was much easier then.

So, how do you get into show business, as the young girl said? You don't "get into" show business. It gets into you! If you can say to yourself, "If I don't make it I can always become a plumber or a car salesman," then ten to one you won't make it. But if you say, "I've got to make it or I'll die!," then you've got it. You'll make it!

CPSIA information can be obtained at www.ICGtesting.com
Printed in the USA
BVOW030808231112

306319BV00004B/10/P